How Many Fish?

MY FIRST
I Can Read Book®

How Many Fish?

story by **Caron Lee Cohen**

pictures by **S. D. Schindler**

HarperCollinsPublishers

HarperCollins®, 📙®, and I Can Read Book®
are trademarks of HarperCollins Publishers Inc.

How Many Fish?
Text copyright © 1998 by Caron Lee Cohen
Illustrations copyright © 1998 by S. D. Schindler
Printed in the U.S.A. All rights reserved.

Library of Congress Cataloging-in-Publication Data
Cohen, Caron Lee.
  How many fish? / story by Caron Lee Cohen ; pictures by S. D. Schindler.
    p.   cm. — (My first I can read book)
  Summary: A school of fish and a group of children frolic in the bay.
  ISBN 0-06-027713-0. — ISBN 0-06-027714-9 (lib. bdg.)
  [1. Fishes—Fiction.   2. Counting.   3. Stories in rhyme.]   I. Schindler, S. D., ill.
II. Title.   III. Series.
PZ8.3.C66Ho   1998
[E]—dc21   97-14512
                                                                 CIP
                                                                 AC

4   5   6   7   8   9   10
❖

For Ruth Stern,
who knows how many fish it takes.
—C.L.C.

How many fish?
How many fish?

6

Six little fish in the bay.

Where do they go?

Why do they go?

8

Six little fish on their way.

How many feet?

How many feet?

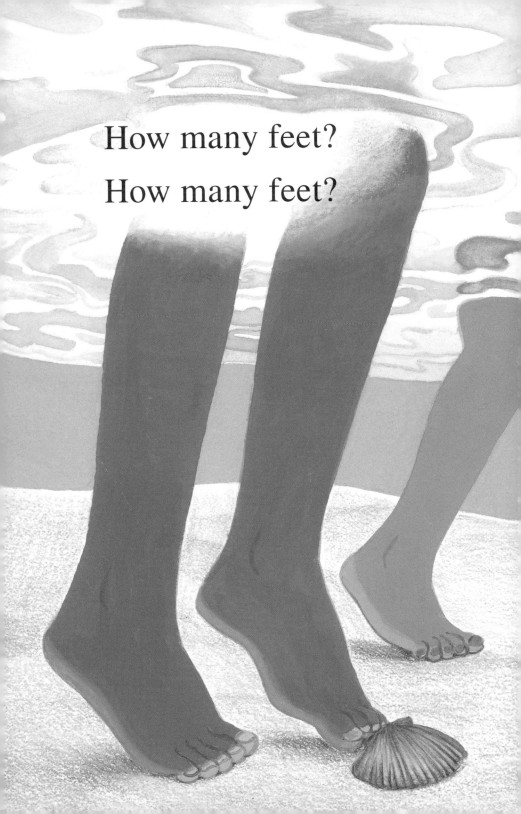

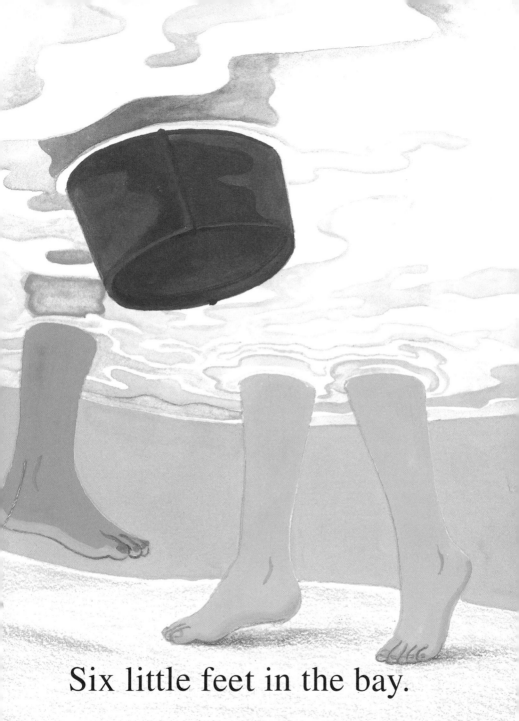

Six little feet in the bay.

Where do they go?

Why do they go?

Six little feet on their way.

How many fish?

How many fish?

14

One yellow fish in the bay.

Where's yellow fish?
Where's yellow fish?

16

Poor yellow fish lost its way.

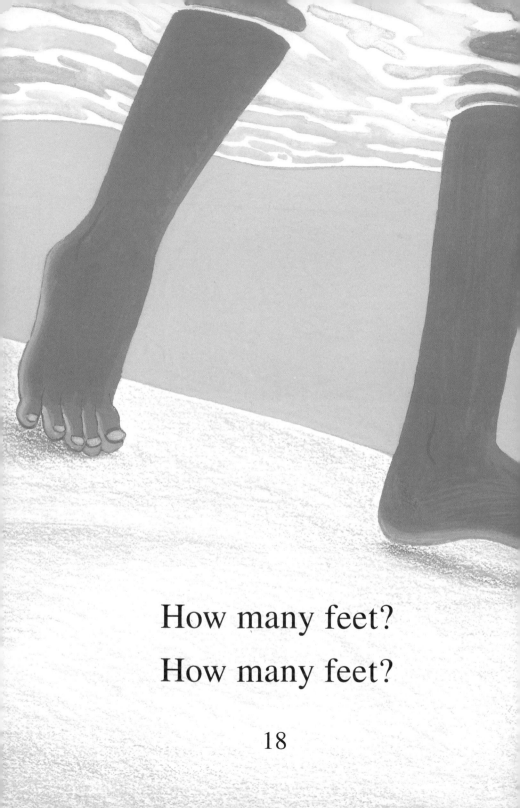

How many feet?

How many feet?

18

Two little feet in the bay.

19

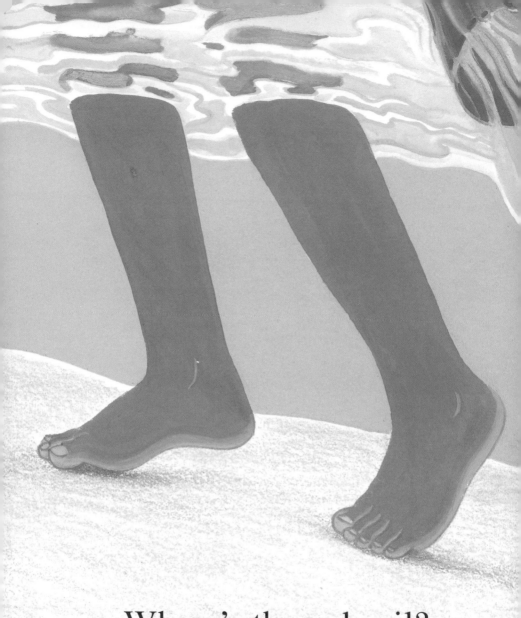

Where's the red pail?

Where's the red pail?

Two little feet dash away.

One happy fish.

One happy fish.

One happy fish on its way!

How many fish?

How many fish?

Six little fish in the bay!

350

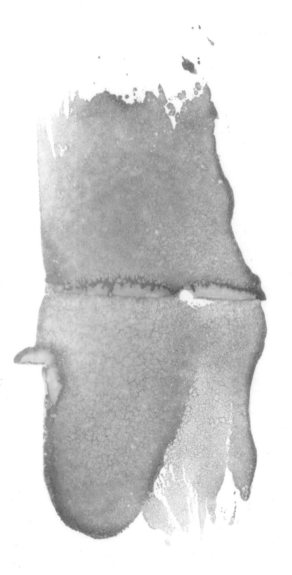

DEAR MISS DEMEANOR

DEAR MISS DEMEANOR

JOAN HESS

St. Martin's Press • New York

Design by Amy Bernstein

Library of Congress Cataloging-in-Publication Data

Hess, Joan.
  Dear Miss Demeanor.

  I. Title.
PS3558.E79785D4   1987   813'.54   87-4436
ISBN 0-312-00702-7

First Edition

10 9 8 7 6 5 4 3 2 1

Dear Miss Demeanor,
  How far should a girl go on the first date?

Dear Reader,
  On the first date, a girl should go as far as Okie's Hamburger Mecca. She should then order french fries. If she paces herself well, the final fry will be consumed five minutes before curfew. Once on the front porch, she may shyly allow masculine lips to be brushed across her cheek before fleeing inside to telephone Miss Demeanor with all the juicy details.

Dear Miss Demeanor,
  My old lady won't put out. Should I dump her and find someone else?

Dear Reader,
  A proper lady will put out the garbage, put out the cat, or, with adequate equipment, put out a forest fire. That is what you meant, isn't it? Perhaps the lady in question lacks asbestos boots.

Dear Miss Demeanor,
  If a married man is seen with a woman at the Xanadu Motel, should someone tell his wife?

Dear Reader,
  Let us presume it was his wife. In any case, what were you doing at the Xanadu Motel?

"O"N"E"

Caron and Inez skittered into the Book Depot like bumper cars gone berserk. Caron's cheeks were scarlet, either from the exertion or, as I suspected, some new bout of outraged indignation. With fourteen-year-olds, indignation is a daily affair. With my daughter, it approaches an hourly schedule.

Caron is all red hair, freckles, and frowns. As an enfant terrible, her imaginary friends were all mischievous imps who knocked over lamps and terrorized the cat. Inez is quite the opposite; she may have been an imaginary friend. Her pale, blurred face hardly ever flushes, and her eyes are too deeply hidden by thick lenses to flash with fury, unbridled or otherwise. She did, however, shove back her stringy brown bangs with a gesture that neared irritation.

I eyed them with an instinctive wariness. "What's up?"

Caron slammed her books down. "You must Do Something, Mother!"

"You really must, Mrs. Malloy," Inez added over Caron's shoulder. She had not yet learned to speak in capital letters, but it was only a matter of time. Caron is an excellent tutor in the delicate art of adolescent melodrama.

"What must I do?" I asked mildly.

"It is absolutely Terrible!" Caron said, beginning to stomp up and down the bookshop aisles. "The situation is absurd, absurd,

absurd! Poor Miss Parchester would never Dream of doing what—what they said she did. She is a Lady!"

Inez bobbled her head earnestly. "That's right, Mrs. Malloy. Miss Parchester is above reproach."

It was, as usual, mystifying. I raised an eyebrow, but as I opened my mouth to protest that I personally had not accused Miss Parchester of anything, a deafening roar shattered the relative tranquillity. A two-hundred-pound woodpecker tearing through the roof. A locomotive coming down the aisle. An ocean liner docking in the living room. Or, foregoing whimsy, a jackhammer a few yards from the door of my bookstore.

I buried my face in my hands as the noise continued to pulsate through every inch of my body. Caron and Inez gaped at each other, by necessity speechless. Just as I thought my head would explode, the roar stopped.

"The street crew," I said, rubbing my temples.

Caron went to the door and peered out. "What on earth is going on, Mother?"

"Powers that be have decided to take up the railroad tracks in the middle of the street, since the last train went through Farberville twenty years ago. Although I cannot fault the sentiment, the noise is driving me crazy! Didn't you see the—"

"I am too worried about Miss Parchester to concern myself with street crews," Caron interrupted. "You have to do something, Mother, before she has a Nervous Breakdown." Inez punctuated the sentiment with a sniffle.

I looked out the window as I formulated a response to their incomprehensible demand. The jackhammer man was rubbing his hands together as he studied his instrument. The gloat on his face brought to mind images of satanic Spanish inquisitors positioning their racks. Caron was right. I did have to do something.

I shooed the girls outside, locked the door, and hung a flyspecked sign on the doorknob. Until Thurber Street was once again a peaceful path to the campus, the Book Depot was closed.

A week or two without an income was cheaper than a hearing aid or a trip to the butterfly farm. There were a few minor matters, such as overdue rent, groceries, Caron's allowance, and payments to the great plastic factory (I never left home without it), but I wouldn't make any money until the crew left. My clientele was too genteel to climb over sawhorses to seek literature. Or semipornographic paperback thrillers, for that matter. Somewhere in Farberville a banker sighed; I felt the icy breeze on the back of my neck, but there wasn't much to do about it.

We walked up the hill. Caron and I live in an upstairs apartment across from the Farber College campus. Although I never before considered it an especially serene location, it was a cemetery in comparison to the construction site in front of the Book Depot. The sorority girls next door produced squeals, but never machine-gun fire.

I took two aspirin, made a cup of tea, and went into the living room. "Who's Miss Parchester?"

Caron's lower lip began to inch forward. "She *was* the journalism teacher at the high school, before He told her that she was fired. I had her for Journalism I, and when Rosie got mononucleosis, Miss Parchester let me take over the column."

"What column?" I asked. Inevitably, it took a while to elicit coherence from Caron, but I was used to it. Motherhood has been with me for fourteen years, although it has crystallized in the last three. Razor-sharp edges and all. The dreaded developmental stage called the terrible twos has nothing over the traumatic teens.

"The Miss Demeanor column," Inez said weakly. I had to search the room for her; she was invisible on the upholstery, like a transparent plastic cover.

"Misdemeanor?" I said. "Is this some sort of legal advice to potential juvenile delinquents? Are you really qualified to—"

"Miss Demeanor!" Caron enunciated the consonants with little sputters of irritation. "An advice column about manners and proper behavior. The students write letters about dating, eating in restaurants, and so on."

My jaw dropped in spite of my efforts to control it. "And you're giving advice about proper behavior? When did you turn into Farberville's Emily Post?"

"When Rosie got mono, Mother; I explained that already. I was Rosie's freshman assistant. Freshmen aren't allowed to be on the newspaper staff, but Miss Parchester thought I could handle Rosie's column until she comes back to school." Caron fluffed her curls and shot me a beatific smile. "Mono can last as long as six months."

"So you're writing the column? You're in charge of etiquette at Farberville High School?"

"I *was* doing the column, but now the *Falcon Crier* has been canceled for the rest of the year. That's why you have to Do Something." The smile vanished as her chin began to quiver, and tears welled in her eyes. I was not impressed, but Inez hurried over to pat the tragic figure's tremulous shoulder.

"It is unjust, Mrs. Malloy," she said in a low voice. "Miss Parchester has been accused of embezzling money from the journalism accounts. I think she's just on some kind of leave, but *he* said that she couldn't even come to school until the account was audited and the money replaced. Poor Miss Parchester was distraught."

"I'm sure she was," I said. "Who's this ominous 'he' you keep mentioning?"

Caron and Inez widened their eyes at each other. "Mr. Weiss," they whispered in awed sibilance.

"Who is Mr. Weiss?" My patience was beginning to evaporate. I had a perfectly wonderful mystery novel in the bedroom. The water in the teapot was still hot. I could put myself to bed and bliss.

Caron gulped at my irreverence. "Mr. Weiss is the principal of Farberville High School, Mother."

"Oh," I said wisely, then proceeded to reiterate the bare outlines of their story, which took no time at all. Accounts short, teacher dismissed, newspaper production halted. Career in journalism thwarted in its infancy. "There's not one thing I can do about any of this, girls. I'm not a CPA, and I doubt my opinion will affect Mr. Weiss's decisions. If Miss Parchester would like a discount on paperback romances while she does a prison term, I could—"

"Mother!"

"Mrs. Malloy!"

The squeaks were almost worse than the jackhammer. "Let's be reasonable," I continued. "This is a high school problem. Surely the proper authorities can resolve this, and if Miss Parchester is as innocent as you say, then she will be back shortly, as will the newspaper and all its columns."

"You have to help," Caron said. "You have to investigate and find out who really took the money. Mr. Weiss won't do anything; he thinks Miss Parchester is a thief. By the time he hires a new teacher, Rosie will be over her mono and I won't get to write the Miss Demeanor column until I'm a senior. That'll be years from now. Eons."

"I am a bookseller, not a private eye. I have no idea how to find bugs in the accounts, nor am I in a position to find out who might be behind the heinous crime. I'm sorry about the column, but there is no way I can help Miss Parchester, Miss Demeanor, or the Falcon Crier."

Caron had recovered nicely from her semihysterical state. Slyly smiling, she said, "I told Miss Dort that you would substitute for Miss Parchester. You can snoop around between classes."

I will not elaborate on my unseemly reaction to this astounding announcement. Inez was sent home (she left briskly and gratefully), and Caron and I verbally explored the ramifications of volunteering others without prior permission, among other things. My voice might have peaked upon occasion, but for the most part I kept my temper under admirable restraint. Caron ran through her repertoire of postpubescent poses, including contrite child (ha!), defender of truth, unjustly accused victim, etc.

I had reached a new plateau of rhetorical sarcasm when the telephone rang. Stabbing my finger at Caron to keep her in place, I grabbed the receiver. "What?"

"Mrs. Malloy?" quavered an unfamiliar voice. "This is Emily Parchester. I was wondering—well, hoping—or should I say, praying—that you might be able to visit me for a cup of tea this afternoon? I realize you must be terribly busy, and I would never dream of imposing on a stranger, but I really have nowhere else to turn."

I glared at Caron as I struggled for decorum. "Miss Parchester—from the high school?"

"Formerly of the high school," she said with quiet dignity. A hiccup rather destroyed the effect. "Would you be so kind as to come to my house, Miss Malloy? I must talk to you."

I made a noise that she interpreted as agreement. After she had given me her address and a time, she bleated out a lengthy promise of gratitude and finally hung up. It took me several minutes to uncurl my fingers in order to replace the receiver—and remind myself of the legal repercussions of child abuse.

"Miss Parchester has invited me to a tea party," I told Caron when I could trust myself. "She has some wild idea that I can salvage her reputation and restore her to her position at the high school. Wherever would she get such an idea?"

Caron shrugged modestly. "I told her how you had solved those murders, and convinced her that you would help her. She's a poor old spinster, Mother, and she's all alone in the world. No one at the high school cares about her. If she loses her job, she'll just sit home by herself until she dies." My daughter, the compassionate columnist.

"In that you face the same fate, you'd better clean up your room so that your body will be discovered at some point during decomposition. Then you may clean the bathroom, finish the dishes, and begin your homework. I'm going to a tea party."

"I don't have any homework."

"Do it anyway." I closed the door with more energy than necessary and went down the stairs. To tea. All I needed was a hat and white gloves. Or a mad hatter and a dormouse.

Miss Parchester lived in a white-shingled house in the oldest section of Farberville. At one time, the cream of society sipped iced tea on the wide verandas, and carriages rolled down the tree-lined streets on their way to the charity balls in vanished hotels.

The ancient elm trees were still there, but most of the houses had been subdivided into apartments for Farber students and transient waiters. Bustled ladies had been replaced with T-shirt-clad students armed with frisbees and beer. Subcompacts filled the carriage houses.

My battered hatchback felt no shame. I mentally straightened my hat and pulled on gloves, then went up the brick sidewalk and stopped to read the names taped on the row of black metal mailboxes. Miss Parchester lived in 1-A. Wonderful. As I hesitated, considering a brisk retreat and another discussion with Caron, a pigtailed college girl bounced through the door, sized me up with undue arrogance, and informed me that Miss Parchester lived in the first apartment on the left.

I managed an insincere nod of thanks and went inside to do my distasteful duty. Tea, sympathy, and firmness, I reminded myself in a determined voice. I was neither detective nor substitute teacher. I was a widow who needed to earn a living in order to support a treacherous, locquacious teenager until she could be tucked away in a college dormitory. Preferably at the University of Fairbanks, or Iceland Polytech.

Before my knuckles reached the door, it flew open. A tiny woman with thin white hair looked up at me as if I had just arrived in a chariot drawn by angels. She wore a black dress and a sensible, handmade cardigan. Her feet were covered by shabby pink slippers, a strange combination.

"Mrs. Malloy? How terribly kind of you to come so promptly."

"Miss Parchester, I want to thank you for offering tea, but I want you to realize——"

"Yes, of course," she said, "please come in. Caron—such a sweet child—has told me so much about you. Although she's only a freshman, she shows surprising talent, don't you think?"

She chattered in that vein as she put me on a brocade sofa, then shuffled down a dark hallway. I looked around curiously. The room was oddly shaped, and at last I deduced it had been divided to create another apartment. The ceiling was high, with an elaborate molding and elegant cornices. The windows, too, were high, but shades let in only a dull yellow light. The furniture would have given an antique dealer a stroke on the spot, if he could have seen it without the teetery piles of bleached newspapers, magazines, ancient composition books, and dust. It smelled of camphor—and dust.

Miss Parchester shuffled back in with a tray. Once I was supplied with tea and one of "mother's sugar cookies," she said, "I do so enjoy tea in the afternoon, Mrs. Malloy. The youth of today seem to prefer those vile carbonated drinks, but tea is so refreshing."

So was scotch, but I didn't mention it. "I'm afraid Caron has given you the wrong impression——"

"The tea service belonged to my great-grandmother," she continued blithely, "and has been in the family for nearly a century. My mother used to serve tea to the Judge every afternoon on the veranda, even though he might have preferred a gentleman's drink."

The woman was clearly a teacher, and a pro. I ceded to the inevitable and politely murmured, "The judge?"

"My father, Judge Amos Parchester. He served three terms on the state Supreme Court, although you're too young to have heard of him. His decisions are still noted to this day. He was an ardent defender of constitutional rights, Mrs. Malloy."

"Indeed?" What else could I say?

"Which is why I chose a career in journalism, as you must have guessed. It was, of course, unthinkable for a lady to work for a newspaper, so I chose to instruct our youth. I've taught for forty years at Farberville High School." She hiccuped on the final word, and gave me a bleary look of apology.

Miss Parchester had been nipping at the elderberry wine, I realized uneasily. The afternoon had been veering downhill, but this was more than anyone should have to put up with. I put down my teacup and said, "We need to discuss whatever nonsense Caron told you about me, Miss Parchester. I am not a detective. I am not an accountant. There is no way that I can—"

"I have never been more humiliated in my life than I was this morning, when Mr. Weiss came into my room," she said, dabbing at her cheek with a wispy handkerchief. "He accused me of being a common thief, of stealing money from the department accounts! Judge Parchester is surely rolling in his grave, and poor mama—bless her soul—must be. . . ."

"I cannot help you," I repeated, trying to sound steadfast.

"There must be some error in the books," she said. The flow from her watery blue eyes increased until the handkerchief was sodden. She daintily wrung it into the cup in her lap, tucked it in her cuff, and then continued, "Mr. Weiss refused to allow me to search for a discrepancy, although it must be a simple error on my part. If only you could check the deposit slips to see if they correspond with the entries, then we could determine if I indeed am responsible for this distressing situation. I had planned to retire this spring, you know, so that I could enjoy whatever pleasures I could find within the limits of my teacher retirement fund and what little I've saved. I had hoped to take up watercolor painting, or perhaps take a short bus tour."

In the far corner of my brain, a violin began to play. Visions of pathetically inept landscapes flashed across my eyes. A short bus trip. Miss Parchester sitting in the mausoleum, gradually disappearing under a layer of dust. Drinking from a cracked wine goblet and talking to the judge. The judge answering. A string quartet took up the melody.

I found myself agreeing to check the deposit slips. "But," I added in desperation, "I am not qualified to substitute for you. I have no teaching credentials, and the only thing I've done with a newspaper is read it."

"Miss Dort feels that your literary background is adequate," Miss Parchester said, taking a slug of what I suspected was not straight Lipton. "You do have a degree in English, don't you, dear? The students are quite capable of handling the production of the newspaper; some of them have worked on the staff for two years."

I shook my head. "I cannot—"

"Of course, you can. As the Judge used to say, a healthy attitude can overcome a mountain. You'll be a splendid teacher, Mrs. Malloy."

The teacup was removed from my numb fingers. Somehow or other, I was congratulated for my endeavor, tidied up, and left on the doorstep to ponder the situation—which was clearly out of control. The jackhammer had done it, I told myself morosely as I returned to my car. Brain damage.

I drove home and climbed the stairs, still bewildered by preceding events. Caron looked up as I opened the door, the receiver in her treacherous hands.

"She just came in, Miss Dort," she chirped.

Miss Dort's name had been popping up like a dandelion in recent conversations, but I had no idea who she was.

"Hello," I said, eyeing the liquor cabinet in the kitchen. If Miss Parchester could indulge before five o'clock, then surely I deserved to do the same.

"Mrs. Malloy, this is Bernice Dort at the high school. I'm the vice-principal in charge of administrative services," said a brisk and somehow brittle voice. "I have been informed that you are willing to substitute for Miss Parchester until a permanent replacement can be found—or until the problem is resolved."

I would not have selected the word "willing." Bulldozed, coerced, emotionally blackmailed—but not "willing." I realized I was staring blankly at the receiver and managed to say, "Something like that, yes."

"I shall assume that you are aware substitute teachers receive thirty-eight dollars a day, and that you are familiar with both the standard state and federal withholdings and the obligatory contribution to the teacher retirement fund. Were you certified, Mrs. Malloy, you would receive forty-three dollars a day."

I did a bit of multiplication in my head. "I taught two undergraduate sections of English literature," I suggested tentatively. It would surely take me a week to solve Miss Parchester's problems, which would appease Visa and keep Lean Cuisines in the freezer. The hypothetical banker's breath on my neck seemed warmer.

"I was speaking of the secondary education certification block, not the amateurish attempts of graduate students to earn their assistantships. The fact that you lack proper credentials does pose a problem for me, Mrs. Malloy. It certainly would have been more expedient had you previously filled out an application at the administration office, but I may be able to slip through a backdated STA111. It will entail extra paperwork."

I wondered if I owed her an apology for the extra paperwork.

I wondered if Caron could be boarded with an Eskimo family. I wondered if the jackhammer was all that bad.

"Mrs. Malloy, are you there?"

"Yes, Mrs. Dort, I am here. If the STA111 is too much trouble, I'll be glad to step aside. I'm sure that there are plenty of qualified substitutes——"

"No, there are not. On an average, we require twelve to fifteen substitutes each academic week, and we are always desperate to fill the gaps so that the educational process can continue with minimal disruption. I fear we must both accept the necessity of a little extra work. Now, I'll need your social security number for the W-8, your date of birth, your academic record, and two personal references——anyone who can confirm that you're not an axe-murderer," Miss Dort said.

I produced the information, listening to the sound of an efficient and officious pen scratching on the other end of the line. When we reached the point of two character references, I drew an embarrassing blank.

"Anyone, Mrs. Malloy," Miss Dort prompted me. "Anyone who knows you well enough to attest to your moral standing in the community."

Miss Parchester? Inez? The jackhammer operator who should have worn a black, hooded cape? I could almost hear Miss Dort's mind questioning my moral standing.

"Peter Rosen," I sputtered. "He's the head of the CID."

"The CID? May I presume that is a government agency of some sort?"

"The Criminal Investigation Department of the local police force," I said. "He's a personal friend of mine, and will certainly vouch for me."

"How fascinating." Miss Dort wasn't fascinated. "I'll need one more name, Mrs. Malloy. There surely is at least one more person who can attest to your character, isn't there?"

I finally remembered the name of the sociology professor who lived downstairs and repeated it grimly. If he were asked about me, I hoped he could figure out who I was. Her forms filled, Mrs. Dort assured me that she would stay at school until midnight to process my paperwork, and told me to report to her office at seven-thirty the next morning.

I replaced the receiver and went to find Caron. The door to the bathroom was locked, and I could hear water gushing into the tub. Apparently the sound was loud enough to muffle my comments, in that I received no reply. If the child had any sense, she would remain in the sanctuary of a bubble bath until her toes turned to prunes. I made a face at the door, then went into the kitchen for a much-needed medicinal dose of scotch and a few more aspirins.

Farberville High School is, no doubt, a perfectly lovely place. Caron and approximately five hundred other students attended daily without much uproar. All sorts of dedicated teachers appeared to do their best to instill knowledge in adolescent heads. As far as I knew, no serious crime riddled the campus or precipitated armed guards in the hallways to protect teachers. I had gone to such an institution myself, although it had been a few years. It hadn't been all that bad. The Book Depot was closed until the street was repaired; I really had nothing of any great importance to do in the interim. The money would hardly finance a shopping spree in Paris, but it would very definitely come in handy should Caron and I decide to indulge in madcap, extravagant activities such as eating.

"It's only for a few days," I reminded the ceiling. Why, then, did it have the same ring as life without parole?

A knock at the door saved me from further schizophrenic conversation with the architecture. I found a smiling Peter Rosen on the landing, a bottle of wine tucked under his arm. He put the wine down and spent a few minutes greeting me with great charm.

"What's only for a few days?" he asked, turning on his inno-

cent smile. At one time in our past the smile had enraged me—
but so had his presence. The effect was quite the opposite now.
For the most part.

"You wouldn't believe it," I said. While I took the wine to the
kitchen, I told him the identity of the newest substitute teacher
at the high school, although I omitted any references to the absurd investigation. Peter does not approve of amateur involve-
ment in piddly little puzzles—on principle. This I knew from
experience.

"I was going to suggest we have dinner tomorrow night," he
said, putting on a show of disappointment that would not have
passed muster in a kindergarten pageant. "But I suppose you'll be
home grading papers and devising lesson plans. Perhaps Caron
will be my escort."

When he wished, the man could be as funny as sleet.

"T" "W" "O"

The high school resembled a collection of yellow blocks abandoned on a moth-eaten shag carpet. No ivy or any such traditional nonsense; just jean-clad students exchanging insults and displaying anatomy as they streamed into one of the four double doors. I felt like a first-grader on the first day of school. I did not hold Caron's hand, however; she could not have survived the humiliation.

I was escorted to the central office, introduced to a pimply boy behind the counter, and warned to wait until Miss Dort appeared. Caron then squealed a greeting to Inez and disappeared into the human tidal wave. My pimply baby-sitter eyed me incuriously, picked up a stack of manila envelopes and left. People of all sizes wandered in and out, ignoring me.

I read a poster that warned against smoking on campus, drinking alcoholic beverages on campus, running in the hallways, missing classes without excuse, and a variety of things I hadn't known teenagers were aware of. I then scanned the list of honor graduates from the previous year, the school calendar for the next year, and everything else tacked on the bulletin board. When in doubt, read the directions.

A rabbity little man with oversized glasses scurried into the office. "Are you the new juvenile parole officer?" he gasped, looking thoroughly dismayed. "I haven't done the seven-one-four forms yet, but I do have the nine-thirties from the spring semester."

"I am not the new parole officer," I said gravely.

"Oh, my goodness no!" He disappeared through a door behind the counter. I heard a series of breathless disclaimers drifting out, as though he needed further reassurance of my identity—or lack thereof.

I was edging toward the nearest exit when a tall, unsmiling woman swept into the office. A gray bun was pinned to the top of her head like a mushroom cap, and pastel blue glasses swung on a cord around her neck. There was a hint of a mustache on her decidedly stiff upper lip.

"Mrs. Malloy? I'm Bernice Dort. Sorry to be late, but Mr. Eugenia has made a muddle of his first quarter grades and someone had to explain it again. And again. It's merely a matter of recording grades, according to the code in the manual, on both the computer card and the reporting form, but Mr. Eugenia seems unable to follow the simplest instructions."

"I'm beginning to wonder if I ought to fill in for Miss Parchester," I said, continuing to retreat. An elbow caught me in the back before I reached the doorway.

"Humph!" A large, red-faced man pushed past me to confront Miss Dort. His silver hair had been clipped with military precision, and nary a hair dared to take a tangential angle. His face was florid, and his bulk encased in a severe blue suit and dark tie. "I want Immerman in my office, Bernice—and I want him now. That boy has gone too far! Perkins called this morning to tell me that Immerman had demanded reinstatement of his eligibility!"

"Oh, how dreadful, Mr. Weiss. Immerman has indeed gone too far. I shall have Mr. Finley send him to the office immediately," Miss Dort agreed in a frigid voice. "Mr. Weiss, this is Mrs. Malloy. She's subbing for Miss Parchester until central admin can locate a certified teacher for the journalism department."

Mr. Weiss stopped in midstep, as if an invisible choke collar had been tightened around his neck. Two small, hard eyes bored into me. His mouth curled slightly in what I presumed was meant to be a smile of welcome, but the message was lost.

I fluttered a hand. "Hello."

"Malloy. Aren't you the woman who runs the Book Depot?" he barked in accusation. "Weren't you involved in some sort of police investigation?"

Caron and Inez had every right to be awed. Although I was nearly forty, I felt a rush of heat to my cheeks and had to pinch myself to hold back a whimper. "That's correct," I said. "I assisted the police with a problem involving the Farber College faculty."

"And now you've decided to be a substitute teacher?" he continued, still staring at me as if I tripped into his office under a beanie with a propeller on the top.

Miss Dort cleared her throat. "Mrs. Malloy has offered to help out, Mr. Weiss. You know how difficult it can be to find a substitute six weeks into the semester, so we'll simply have to make do with what we can get. Now, if you'll excuse us, I'll take Mrs. Malloy down to the journalism room and get her settled. Her paperwork is on your desk, although I've already sent the triplicates to central admin."

Mr. Weiss gave her a tight nod. "Then get Immerman in here. Tell his first period teacher that he'll be in my office during class."

Miss Dort seemed on the verge of a heel-clicking salute, but she instead bobbed her head curtly and picked up her clipboard. Thus armed, she led me out of the office and into the battle arena. We marched down several miles of hallway as she rattled off names, departments, and other bits of meaningless information. Students leaped out of our path, and conversations were revived only in our wake.

We then descended into the bowels of the building. A bell jangled shrilly as we reached the bottom step; seconds later students scuttled through doorways like cockroaches caught in the light.

Miss Dort pointed at a scarred door. "That is the old teachers' lounge, Mrs. Malloy. The new one is on the second floor in the west wing; you may find the distance inconvenient. Most of the teachers in the basement still congregate in the old room, but you may use whichever you prefer."

I suspected I would prefer the one with a well-stocked bar. Nineteen minutes had passed since Caron dragged me through the door. Nineteen incredibly long minutes. Seven hours remained in the school day. This scheme was insane. I would personally buy Miss Parchester a pad of watercolor paper and a bus ticket to wherever she desired to go. Caron could accompany her as a porter.

"This," Miss Dort announced as she opened a door, "is the journalism department."

The room resembled the interior of a cave. The air was foul, reminding me of the miasma of a very old garbage can. Miss Dort snorted, switched on a light and gave me a stony look meant to impede flight.

"You do not have a homeroom class, so you will not have to deal with the attendance reports until your first class arrives in seven minutes. Miss Parchester's daily unit delineations will be in a dark-blue spiral notebook, and her rosters in a small black book. Good luck, and keep in mind the faculty motto: TAKE NO PRISONERS." The woman actually started for the door.

"Wait a minute!" I yelped. "What am I supposed to do about—"

"I have to make the daily announcements, Mrs. Malloy. Homeroom will be over in six and one half minutes, and I must remind the students about the variations in the bus route on snow days." She sailed out the door before I could argue.

I did not sink to the floor and burst into tears, although the idea crossed my mind. On the other hand, I did not linger to explore the murky corners of Carlsbad Cavern. I figured I had over five minutes of free time, so I bolted for the teachers' lounge—which had to be more enlightening than any book of daily unit delineations.

The lounge was decorated in early American garage sale. The several sofas were covered with tattered plaid variations that would have convulsed a Scotsman; the formica-topped table was covered with nicks, scratches and stains. There were two rest rooms along one wall, and between them a tiny kitchenette with a refrigerator, soda machine, and—saints be praised—a gurgling coffee pot. A variety of cups hung on a peg board; not one of them said "Malloy" in decorative swirls, or even "Parchester."

The situation was dire enough to permit certain emergency measures, including petty theft. I took down a cup, poured myself a medicinal dose of caffeine and slumped down on a mauve-and-green sofa to brood. Four minutes at the most. Then, if I remembered my high school experiences with any accuracy, students would converge on my cave, their little faces bright with eagerness to learn, their little eyes shining with innocence. Presumably, I would have to greet them and do something to restrain them for fifty minutes or so. Others would follow. Between moments of imparting wisdom, I was supposed to audit the books and expose an embezzler.

In the midst of my gloomy mental diatribe, a woman in a bright yellow dress came into the lounge. She was young, pretty, and slightly flustered by my presence. "Hello, I'm Paula Hart," she said with a warm smile. "Beginning typing and office machines."

"Claire Malloy. Intermediate confusion and advanced despair," I said. My smile lacked her radiance, but she probably knew what daily unit delineations were.

"Are you subbing for Miss Parchester? This whole thing is just unbelievable, and I feel just dreadful about it. Poor Emily would never do such a thing. She must be terribly upset." Miss Hart went into the kitchenette and returned with a cup decorated with pink hearts. "I'm in the room right across from you, Mrs. Malloy. If you need anything, feel free to ask."

I opened my mouth to ask the definition of a delineation when a thirty-year-old Robert Redford walked into the lounge. He was wearing a gray sweatsuit, but it in no way diminished the effect. Longish blond hair, cornflower blue eyes, dimples, compact and well-shaped body. The whole thing, living and breathing. And smiling solely for Paula Hart, who radiated right back. They had no need for physical contact; the space between them shimmered with unspoken messages.

Young love was nice if one liked that sort of thing, but I was more concerned with my personal problems. Before I could suggest they unlock eyes and make constructive comments about my classes, the bell rang. The sound of tromping feet competed with screeches of glee. Locker doors banged open and slammed closed. The war was on, and I couldn't do battle in the lounge.

"Bye," I said as I headed into disaster. Neither of them seemed visibly distressed by my departure—if they noticed.

The journalism room was, as I had feared, filled with students. I went to the desk, dug through the mess until I found a black book, and then tossed it at a pudgy girl with waist-length black hair and a semblance of intelligence.

"Tell everyone to sit down and then take roll," I commanded coolly. If I could only find the other book, I suspected I could discover who they were and why they were there.

The girl goggled briefly but began shouting names above the roar. Eventually the students sat down to eye me in a disconcertingly carnivorous way. I squared my shoulders and reminded myself that they were simply unpolished versions of the species.

We quickly established that they were Beginning Features, and I was a substitute with no interest in their future. They agreed to hold down the noise; I agreed to leave them alone until I found the daily unit delineation book. My pudgy aide at last produced it from a cardboard box beside the desk.

Since we were all content with the present arrangement, I left them to whisper while I scanned the book. Second period was to be Intro to Photo, and third was gloriously free, followed by a reasonable lunch break. Fourth period was *Falcon Crier,* which I presumed had something to do with the newspaper, fifth was Photo II, and sixth was something called "Falconnaire." If I was alive at that point, I could go home.

The whispering grew a bit louder. I turned a motherly frown on them, and the noise obediently abated. Pleased with my success, I wandered around the room, discovering a coat closet filled with old newspapers, boxes of curled photographs, a quantity of dried rubber cement bottles, and a small, inky hole that proved to be a darkroom in all senses of the word. It also proved to be the source of the garbage can aroma. I now knew the confines of my domain, for better or worse.

I was sitting at the desk with an old newspaper when a box on the wall above my head began to crackle. After a moment of what sounded like cellophane being crumpled, a voice emerged.

"Mrs. Malloy, I have neither your attendance list for first period, nor your blue slips. I must have them at the beginning of each period." Miss Dort, or Frosty the Snowman.

I gazed at the box. "So?"

"So I must have them, Mrs. Malloy."

Good heavens, the thing worked both ways. I wondered if she could see me from her mountaintop aerie as well. "I'll send them to the office," I called with a compliant expression, just in case. The box squawked in reply, then fell silent.

Pudge waved a paper at me and left the room. Hoping she knew what she was up to, I returned to an article on the chances of a district championship in football, complete with photographs of neckless boys squinting into the sun, but nevertheless optimistic.

On the last page, I found a photograph of Robert Redford himself. The caption below informed me that this was the new assistant coach, Jerry Finley. He thought the chances for a championship were good if the boys worked hard during practice, perfected their passing game, and gave the team their personal best. He was delighted to be at Farberville High and proud of the Falcons. His hobbies included water-skiing and Chinese cooking. When not on the gridiron, he would be found teaching general science and drivers' ed, or supervising study hall in the cafeteria.

Or dimpling at Miss Hart, I amended to myself.

The bell rang, and the class departed with the stealth of a buffalo herd. Their replacements looked remarkably similiar. I tossed the attendance book to a weedy boy with glasses, made the same announcement about immediate goals, and even managed to send my attendance slip to the office before the box crackled at me.

I spent the period rummaging through Miss Parchester's desk for anything that might contain accounts. I found a year's supply of scented tissues, worn pencils, blue slips whose purpose escaped me, and other teaching paraphenalia. When the bell rang, I went down the hall to the teachers' lounge to drown my sorrows in coffee.

As I opened the door, I heard a furious voice saying, "Mr. Pitts, you are a despicable example of humanity. I have told you repeatedly that you must not—must not—enter the lounge for any reason other than maintenance. I shall have to report you to Mr. Weiss!"

The speaker was a grim-faced woman with hair the color of concrete. On one side of her stood a diminutive sort with bluish hair, on the other a lanky woman whose shoulders barely supported her head. All three wore long dark dresses, cardigans, and stubby heels. They also wore disapproving frowns. Despite minor variations, they were remarkably similar, as if they were standard issue from some prehistoric teachers' college; I had had them or remarkable facsimiles throughout my formative years. Many of said years had been spent cringing when confronted with steely stares and tight-lipped smiles.

The object of their scorn was a man with a broom. His thin black hair glittered in the light from years of accumulated lubrication. He wore dirty khaki pants, a gray undershirt that might have been white in decades past, and scuffed cowboy boots. His lower lip hung in moist and petulant resignation, but his eyes flittered to me as if to share some secret amusement. Having nothing in common with lizards, I eased behind the three women and slipped into the kitchenette.

"Well, Mr. Pitts," the woman boomed on, "it is obvious that you have been rummaging in the refrigerator once again. Stealing food, contaminating the lunches of others, and generally behaving like a scavenger. I am disgusted by the idea of your filthy fingers in my food! Disgusted, Mr. Pitts! Have you nothing to say in your defense?"

"I didn't even open the refrigerator," he growled. "I ain't been in here since yesterday evening when I cleaned. You don't have no reason to report me, Mrs. P."

"My coffee cup is missing, Mr. Pitts. The evidence is clear."

Oh, dear. I stuck my head out the door and pasted on an angelic smile. "I'm afraid I may be the cup culprit. I was in earlier and borrowed one of them."

Three sets of eyes turned to stare at me. The middle woman said, "We do not borrow cups from each other. It is unhygienic." On either side of her, heads nodded emphatically.

"I'm sorry, but there were no extra cups. I'll wash it out immediately and return it to you," I said, trying to sound composed in the face of such unanimous condemnation.

"There is no detergent," the woman said. "I'll have to take it to the chemistry room and rinse it out with alcohol." She held out her hand.

I meekly gave her the cup and babbled further apology as the three marched out of the room. Once they were gone, I sank down on a sofa and lectured myself on the ephemerality of the situation.

"Who're you supposed to be?" the lizard snickered.

"I'm the substitute for Miss Parchester in the journalism room."

"I'm Pitts, the custodian. I used to be a janitor, but they changed my title. Didn't pay any more money, though. Just changed the title to custodian 'cause it sounds more professional. I had hopes of being a building maintenance engineer, but Weiss wouldn't go for it."

"How thrilling for you," I said, closing my eyes to avoid looking at him. I immediately became aware of an odor that topped anything in the journalism room. Decidedly more organic, and wafting from the custodian's person. I decided to risk everything and steal another cup; coffee held squarely under my nose might provide some degree of masking.

Pitts leered at me as I went into the kitchen and randomly grabbed a cup. "You stole Mrs. P.'s cup awhile ago, didn't you?" he called. "She was gonna have my hide, but she's always trying to get something on me. I'm beginning to think she doesn't like me—ha, ha."

I couldn't bring myself to join in the merriment, so I settled for a vague smile. I returned to the sofa and tried to look pensive. Pitts watched me for a few minutes, then picked up a bucket and ambled into the ladies room, his motives unknown.

The lounge door opened once more. A man and woman came in, laughing uproariously at some private joke. The man was dressed in tweeds, complete with leather elbow patches. His light brown hair was stylishly trim and his goatee tidy. My late husband had been a college professor, and I was familiar with the pose. I wryly noted the stem of a pipe poking out of his coat pocket.

The woman had no aspirations to the academic role. Her black hair tumbled down to her shoulders, and her makeup was more than adequate for a theater stage or a dark alley. She wore a red dress and spike heels. She was dressed for a gala night on the town. At eleven-thirty in the morning, no less.

The two filled coffee cups (I hadn't stolen theirs, apparently) and came in to study me.

"*Cogito, ergo sum* Sherwood Timmons," the man said with a deep bow. "Or I think that's who I am. Who might you be?"

"Claire Malloy, for Miss Parchester."

The woman's smile vanished. "I'm Evelyn West, French. In case you missed it, Sherwood's Latin—and other dead languages. We're all so upset about Emily's forced vacation. Weiss was rash to assume her errors were intentional."

"Anything Weiss does must be taken *cum grano salis,*" Sherwood added as he sat down across from me. "So you're our newest of our little gang, Claire. How are you doing with the *profanum vulgus?*"

Evelyn kicked him, albeit lightly. "Sherwood has a very bad habit of thinking himself amusing when he lapses into Latin. I've tried to convince him that he's merely insufferable, but he continues to torment us." She added something in French. Although I do not speak the language, the essential profanity of it was unmissable. He laughed, she laughed, we all laughed. Even Pitts, who had slithered out of the ladies room, made a croaking noise.

"Hiya, Mr. Timmons, Miz West," he added in an obsequious voice. "Say, Mrs. P. is mad at me again, but I didn't do nothing. Could you see if you could maybe stop her before she goes to Mr. Weiss?"

"Part of the reason she's upset is that you did precisely nothing last night, including clean the classroom floors, empty the trashcans, or wipe down the chalkboards. It's beginning to disturb even me, Pitts, and I vowed on my grandmother's grave that I would be kind to children and dumb animals."

"*Quis custodiet ipsos custodes?*" Sherwood murmured.

Pitts smirked. "I like that, Mr. Timmons. What does it mean?"

"Who will guard the guards themselves. In your case, Arm Pitts, it loosely refers to who might be induced to clean the unclean."

Pitts snatched up his tools of the trade. "That ain't funny, Mr. Timmons. It's not easy to keep this place clean, you know. The students aren't the only dirty people around here. Some of the teachers ain't too sanitary—especially in their personal lives." He stomped out of the lounge, muttering to himself.

"Arm Pitts?" I inquired, wrinkling my nose.

Evelyn began to fan the air with a magazine. "Rather hard to miss the allusion, even in Latin. Pitts is a horrid, filthy man; no one can begin to fathom why Weiss allows him to keep the job. The supply room is around the corner from the lounge, and rumor has it that Pitts has enough hooch to open a retail liquor store. The cigarette smoke is thick enough to permeate the walls. Who knows what he peddles to some of our less innocent students while Weiss conveniently looks the other way."

"Tell me about Mr. Weiss," I suggested. If for no other reason, I needed to know the enemy.

"Herbert Weiss," Sherwood said, "is a martinet of the worst ilk. The man has the charm of a veritable *anguis in herba*."

"Sherwood," Evelyn began ominously, "you—"

"A snake in the grass," he translated, a pitying smile twitching the tip of his goatee. "In any case, Farberville High has survived more than ten years of his reign of terror, but this year he has become noticeably *non compos mentis*—to the *maximus*."

"That's true," Evelyn added. "I've been here four years, and I have noticed a change for the worse this fall. In the past, Weiss has remained behind his office door, doing God knows what but at least avoiding the staff. Now he roams the hall like Hamlet's daddy, peering into classrooms, interfering with established procedure, and generally paying attention to things he has never before bothered with."

"Perhaps he's up for a promotion," I said. "Often that produces an attempt at efficiency."

"We've toyed with that theory," Sherwood said. "Of course, that means we'd have Miss Dort as the captain of our ship. In any case, I shall escape through my muse."

"Sherwood is writing the definitive work on parallels between the primitive forest deities and the Bible," Evelyn said. "If he can get it published, he hopes to scurry into an ivy tower and teach those who strive for a modicum of academic pretentions."

The author stiffened. "I've had some interest shown by several university presses. My manuscript is well over a thousand pages now, but I hope to complete it for formal submission before the end of this semester. It is, and I speak modestly, *sui generis*. In a class by itself."

When Sherwood the infant had lisped his first word, it hadn't been modestly. However, I found the two amusing and civilized, especially in comparison to the others. I inquired about the woman whose coffee cup I had stolen.

"So you've met the Furies on your travels," Sherwood said gleefully. "Alecto, Tisiphone and Megaera apply their stings to those who have escaped public retribution. Guardians of the FHS code of morality, our dear Eumenides."

"They don't like Sherwood," Evelyn said with a shrug. "They suspect him of saying rude things, but none of them understands Latin. They're right, of course."

On that note, the Furies trooped into the lounge in a precise vee formation. The coffee cup was presumably sterile, its owner assured that my germs would not mingle with her own. But from their expressions (cold and leery), they were not sure that I wouldn't pull another vile prank in the immediate future.

Evelyn said, "This is Claire Malloy, who is subbing for Emily. Claire, this is Mrs. Platchett, chairman of the business department. On her left, Miss Bagby, who teaches sophomore biology, and on her right, Miss Zuckerman, who teaches business."

I stood up in an attempt to elicit forgiveness. "I'm pleased to meet you, and I'm truly sorry about using the coffee cup."

Mrs. Platchett remained unmoved by my gesture. "As Mae can tell you, certain microbes can cause great distress for those of us with delicate constitutions, although the carrier can remain unaffected. Will you be able to bring a cup from home, or shall I use our little lounge fund to purchase one for you?"

"I'll bring one tomorrow." It seemed time for a new subject. "So you teach with Paula Hart? I met her here during the homeroom period."

"Miss Hart's class was unusually rowdy this morning," Mrs. Platchett said in an icy voice. "I should have realized she was remiss in her homeroom obligations. It is hardly surprising to learn she was not even there."

The thin woman flared her nostrils in sympathy. "I noticed the noise across the hall, Alexandria, but I assumed Miss Hart was doing her inept best to control the class. It is often impossible to teach over the uproarious laughter from her room."

Typing wasn't all that much fun, but I didn't point that out. Nor did I mention the lovers' tryst that was obviously scheduled in advance for optimum privacy.

Sherwood stood up and straightened his tie. "Pitts said you were on his case, Alexandria. Did you follow through or was it an idle threat?"

"I shall presume, Mr. Timmons, that you are asking if I spoke to Mr. Weiss about Pitts's shameful neglect of the basement classrooms. I did, although Mr. Weiss seemed unimpressed. He did agree to have a word with the man, but I doubt we shall see a substantial improvement in the future."

Evelyn joined Sherwood in the doorway. "The only word that might help would be 'fired.' In the meantime, I have a portable vacuum cleaner that I'll gladly share."

Sherwood bowed. "In any case, ladies, *carpe diem*. Or to translate loosely in accordance with the current debasement of the English language, have a nice day." With a wink, he strolled out of the lounge.

"T"H"R"E"E"

For the next fifty minutes, I huddled on the mauve-and-green sofa, trying to provoke appendicitis or something equally time-consuming. The best I could do was a sneeze, hardly worthy of hospitalization.

The Furies took plastic containers from the refrigerator and settled around the formica table. Mrs. Platchett opened hers warily, as if suspecting it had been booby-trapped to explode.

"It seems to be untouched," she sniffed after a lengthy examination. "If Pitts has been poking in it, he left no fingerprints."

The diminutive one gave the contents of her container the same careful scrutiny. "Mine appears intact, also, but I doubt that carrot sticks and broccoli spears might take fingerprints. The idea is enough to induce nausea, Alexandria. I'm not at all sure I can eat today."

"Nonsense, Tessa! You must eat, and you know it. Your doctor was most precise in the dietary orders." Mrs. Platchett picked up a sandwich, and they all began to chew the precise number of times for optimum digestibility. Termites do the same thing, I understand, but more quietly.

Paula Hart came by and offered to share her salad with me. Preferring to remain the martyr to the very end—and unsure if lettuce took fingerprints—I declined, and she left to munch greens in more congenial surroundings, or to peel grapes for the assistant coach with the dimples. Chomping steadily, the Furies failed to acknowledge her brief appearance.

I finally decided to return to the cave to sulk without sound effects. As I rose, Miss Dort darted into the lounge. "Here you are, Mrs. Malloy. I went by the journalism room, but you were not there."

I certainly couldn't argue with that. "I was on my way there," I said. "The daily unit delineation book is more thrilling than a gothic romance, and I wanted to settle down with it for a few minutes before the next class."

Miss Dort perched her glasses on her nose to peer at me. "Indeed, Mrs. Malloy. I wanted to remind you to turn in your blue slips with your attendance slips each period. They are vital." She went into the kitchenette and came out with a square plastic box. "So sorry I can't eat with you ladies today. The paperwork is piled sky-high on my desk, and of course I must prepare for the arrival of the auditors from the state Department of Education."

Mrs. Platchett washed down a masticated mouthful. "Bernice, I want you to realize how distressed I am by this sordid affair. Emily is quite innocent; she would never touch a penny of the school's money. The idea is preposterous."

The one I thought was Mae Bagby nodded. "Emily Parchester has served the students of Farberville High School for forty years, and her reputation remained unblemished until yesterday."

The third Fury, who had dozed off, opened her eyes to add her support. "Her father was Judge Amos Parchester of the state Supreme Court, Bernice. That bears comment."

Miss Dort could read the storm signals as well as I. "The auditors will see," she murmured as she started out the door. She halted and looked at me over her shoulder. "Teachers meeting this afternoon, three-thirty in the cafetorium."

"What?" I sputtered. I had other plans for that time. I fully intended to be on the heels of the last student out the door. If I was agile enough, I might be on his toes.

Three heads swiveled to stare at me. "We always have a teachers meeting the third Thursday of the month," Mrs. Platchett informed me coldly. "It is a tradition that has survived for a very long time at Farberville High School." And no whippersnapper was going to disrupt it if she had any say in the matter.

I did not care if she had ridden a brontosaurus to the first meeting. I cared about escape, a hot bath, and a world populated by adults with minimal interest in education. I opened my mouth to protest, but Miss Dort had sailed away to her paperwork, smug in the knowledge that I was neatly trapped. I rather wished I knew a Latin expletive; my Anglo-Saxon ones would have caused a three-cornered swoon.

The bell rang in the middle of my decorous growl. I ambled down the hallway in time to shoo a few stragglers into the cave, then forced myself to follow them. My darling daughter was perched on the desk like a leprechaun on a toadstool.

"How's it going, Mother?" she chirped.

I pushed her off the desk and pointed at a girl with frizzy hair. "You, what's your name?"

"Bambi McQueen, Mrs. Malloy."

"On your birth certificate?"

"Yes, ma'am. I'm the student editor for the *Falcon Crier,* and your fourth-period aide."

I tossed the roster book to her. "Take role, send in the attendance slip and the little blue things, and then tell everybody what to do."

"But, Mrs. Malloy, if the newspaper isn't going to come out next week, then I don't know what to tell everybody. Should we just read or something, or should we go ahead and do assignments for the paper anyway?"

I glared at Caron as I spoke to the cervine whiner. "I don't care what you do, Bambi. I hope not to be here more than a few days; thus I have no interest in your academic progress, the next issue of the newspaper, or your interim activities. Think of something to amuse yourselves."

The candor perplexed her. She chewed on her lower lip for a long minute, gauging the potential limits. "Maybe some of us should go to the printer's to let him know that the newspaper won't come out as scheduled?" she suggested.

I flipped a hand. "By all means, let us not keep the poor man in suspense."

Bambi and ten eager volunteers dashed for the door. When we were alone, Caron flopped down in a desk. "That was dumb, Mother. They just wanted to leave the campus; they could have called the printer. Seniors!"

"They may drive to the West Coast, for all I care. I have to devise a way to avoid a barbaric tradition known as a teachers meeting—this afternoon after school."

"What about Miss Parchester? Have you figured out who framed her yet?"

"I have been here slightly more than five hours. For some inexplicable reason, students keep appearing in the room in droves, expecting to be supervised if not regaled with mature insights. An opportunity to figure out who, if anyone, framed Miss Parchester has not yet arisen. I need an excuse to avoid the teachers meeting."

"Have you met Mr. Weiss or any of the teachers?" Caron said without a flicker of sympathy for my plight. The child knew nothing of meetings; her day would come. Of death, taxes, and committees, I preferred the first two.

I ran through the list of those I had encountered during the morning. When I mentioned Miss Hart and her coach, Caron interrupted with a noisy sigh.

"Aren't they the cutest couple? Miss Hart used to date Mr. Timmons, but he wouldn't marry her so she could have babies.

When she saw Coach Finley, it was love at first sight, and now everyone except Mr. Timmons knows that they're secretly engaged." More sighs.

"How do you know all this?"

"This is a school, not a monastery, Mother. Do you want to hear what Mr. Timmons said when he found out that Miss Hart was dating Coach Finley? It was in Latin, but it was still dirty."

"No, I don't. This zoo may be a microcosm of society, but I have no desire to delve into its social interactions." I sat down behind the desk and produced a few sighs of my own. "I suppose I'll have to stay after school for this silly meeting. You can go home and cook dinner."

"But what about the newspaper—and Miss Parchester?"

There was that. I shrugged and said, "The accounts are not here; Miss Dort must have them in her office. Even if I had some idea of what to do with them—and I don't—I haven't seen them. I don't know the procedure for depositing money or writing checks to pay bills."

Caron gathered up her books and purse. "Ask Miss Hart. She's the cheerleader and drill-team sponsor, the business club sponsor and the senior class advisor, so she deals with oodles of club accounts. I'm going to the library, Mother." She left with the briskness of a Dort.

I picked up a copy of the *Falcon Crier* from the previous month and flipped through the pages. Miss Demeanor was on the second page, which was dated October 22.

Dear Miss Demeanor,
  My boyfriend wants to take me to a fancy French restaurant for our one-month anniversary. He wants to order champagne, but the waiter probably won't serve us. What should we do—walk out?

Dear Reader,
  Miss Demeanor must sympathize. Coq au vin does not go well

with coke au cola. However, Miss Demeanor prefers to cater to her stomach before she caters to her sense of injustice. Eat, pay the bill, and then walk out. That will show 'em.

Dear Miss Demeanor,
    Two boys have asked me to the homecoming dance next week, and I don't know which one to say yes to. One of them has pimples, but he also has a neat car. The other one is really foxy, but he barfed on my dress at the September Mixer. I'm not sure I'd feel safe with him anywhere near. Besides, I have a really nifty new dress. What do you think?

Dear Reader,
    How much did the dress cost? How much did the neat car cost? How much will the dry cleaners cost? If you can't figure it out, sign up for general math.

Dear Miss Demeanor,
    The reason I was at the Xanadu Motel was because I was following the married man. His wife has brown hair, but the woman he was with didn't. What do you think about that?

Dear Reader,
    Nothing at all. Why should I? For that matter, why should you? There are at least three people more qualified than either of us to ponder the situation.

Puzzled, I folded the *Falcon Crier* and stuffed it into Miss Parchester's middle drawer. The first two letters sounded like typical adolescent stuff, but the third had an edge that neared nastiness. I wondered why Miss Demeanor had bothered with it. I wondered where the Xanadu Motel was, and who would want to go there. I then dismissed the muddle to wonder if there were any way to disappear at three-thirty without risking the wrath of Bernice Dort.

The bell rang once again, and shortly thereafter the room swelled with Photo II, a.k.a. the newspaper photographers. We exchanged the necessary courtesies and they managed to talk among themselves until the class was over. Ho hum. Teaching wasn't all that hard.

My last (thank God) class was the mysterious "Falconnaire." Although I was less than frantic for an explanation, I was mildly curious. Once the dozen or so students were seated, I asked them.

"The Falconnaire is the yearbook," said a blond girl with the body of a lingerie model. Her blouse did little to discourage the comparison; buttons were nearly bursting out all over. She made no effort to hide a broad yawn as she added, "I don't think we can do anything until they find a replacement for our embezzling teacher."

"What's your name?" I said peevishly. Now I was going to have to withstand the compulsion to yawn for fifty minutes.

"Cheryl Anne Weiss," she said. When I failed to react with any visible astonishment, she produced a pout of superiority. "My father happens to be the principal of Farberville High School."

"That's right," grunted a hulking form in the back of the room. "Cheryl Anne's daddy is the king of this dump. She's kinda like a princess."

I tried a stern, teacherish frown. "What's your name—Prince Albert?"

"Theodore Immerman, ma'am; everybody calls me Thud. I'm in charge of the sports section of the yearbook, if there is a yearbook. Are you gonna take Parchester's place and tell us what to do, or just take the rest of the money?" Smirk, smirk.

"Why are you so sure Miss Parchester is guilty, Mr. Immerman? Isn't it possible that there was a simple error on someone's part?"

His massive shoulders rose like snowy Alps. "I don't know, ma'am. I just know she had the checkbook, and now the money is gone. I sure as hell didn't write myself any bonuses."

The class tittered nervously, but Thud seemed pleased with his little joke. It was, I decided, in keeping with his intellectual capacity. A girl in the front row murmured that they could continue to organize the layout of the sophomore pictures, even though Miss Parchester was not available to supervise them.

I rewarded her with the roster, instructed the class to busy themselves with the layout of said pictures, and went to the cabinet to find more copies of the *Falcon Crier*. The Miss Demeanor column was quite clever for a postpubescent mind, although I wasn't sure if the ailing Rosie had written the examples before her quarantine, or if my daughter had done so. The coq au vin was a bit startling; the only chicken Caron had eaten at my dining-room table arrived in a cardboard bucket, an original recipe but not of mine.

Before I could dig out a copy of the newspaper, an argument broke out on one side of the room. Cheryl Anne Weiss was not happy with darling Thud, nor he with her.

"I can't do it!" the blond girl squealed. Her ponytail swung around her head to flop across her eyes, and she swung it back with a practiced hand and an equally practiced scowl.

"You said you could, dammit!" Thud thundered. "You swore that he wouldn't yank my eligibility!"

"He won't listen to me, Thud. I tried as hard as I could, but now I don't know what to do. I'll think of something else."

I slammed the cabinet door to get their attention. "Excuse me for disturbing you, but the discussion will have to be postponed until after class. I left my whistle at home."

Thud's simian brow sank until his eyes were barely visible, and his lips crept out. Cheryl Anne, on the other hand, gave him an impertinent sneer and flounced back to her desk. The ponytail and other things wiggled with disdain. The rest of the students resumed their whispers, feigning no interest whatsoever in the argument.

I decided to forego the newspaper and spent the rest of the period preventing a holocaust in the cave. Thud and Cheryl Anne exchanged numerous dark looks and made numerous inarticulate and threatening noises, but restrained themselves from further verbal combat. I kept the maternal frown on full power until the bell finally rang and I could send them away. As the two met in the doorway, they resumed their argument. I could hear them all the way down the hall, but I didn't care. It was three-twenty-five.

The cafetorium was at the far end of the first floor. I found a seat toward the rear, smiled vaguely at those around me, and prepared for utter tedium. Other teachers looked equally excited. The Furies marched in and took possession of the front row; Miss Hart and Coach Finley slipped in to sit in the row behind me. Evelyn and Sherwood joined me seconds later, looking like naughty children who had come straight from the cookie jar. Sherwood bowed slightly and gave me a broad wink.

Mr. Weiss strode to the front of the room, with Miss Dort on his tailwind. He snapped at her to take attendance (to whom would she send it?) and glowered until she made her way from "Aaron" to a final "Zuckerman." All were present.

"This will be short and to the point," he barked. "Item one: the schedule for Homecoming activities is on the mimeograph Miss Dort will distribute, along with the names of dance chaperones and stadium-concession supervisors. There will be no changes, tradeoffs, or excuses. If your name is there, be there. Thirty minutes early."

Miss Dort snapped to attention and passed out the pale purple mimeographs, eyeing us challengingly. When she arrived in the rear, she curled her lips at me. "You'll cover for Parchester at the dance, Mrs. Malloy," she whispered with the expression of a barracuda swimming alongside a cellulitic snorkler. I managed a nod.

Mr. Weiss tapped his foot until Miss Dort finished her chore and scurried back to his side. "Item two: the auditors will be here next week to examine every club ledger, along with the journalism account and our general accounts. I want records in my office tomorrow morning before home room. I want copies of expenditures for the previous year. I want a list of deposits and checks for this semester—in duplicate. Your books had better balance to the last cent. No excuses."

A groan went down the rows, and a particularly unhappy one from Miss Hart behind me. According to Caron, she had oodles of accounts. No hot date that night. From Sherwood Timmons came a barely audible, "*Quem Deus vult perdere, prius dementat*—those whom the Gods wish to destroy, they first make mad. The man's a veritable draconian these days."

"Any questions?" Mr. Weiss said, looking over our heads.

Paula Hart raised her hand. "Mr. Weiss, the seniors are frantic to know what will happen with the yearbook. Several of the girls actually burst into tears in my room because they're so worried they won't have a memento of their final year."

To my surprise, Mr. Weiss did not roar at the insubordination. He located Miss Hart in the corner and smiled with all the sincerity of an airport missionary. "I have not reached a decision about the Falconnaire. The seniors would be concerned, naturally." He tugged on his chin, then glanced at Miss Dort. "Tell the substitute—ah, the Malloy woman—to get on with the yearbook, Bernice. Miss Hart and I wouldn't want our senior class to be disappointed, would we?"

"Wait a minute," the Malloy woman yelped. "I have no idea how to 'get on' with the yearbook. I don't make books; I sell them. They come ready made."

"The Falconnaire staff can handle it," Miss Dort said firmly.

Paula Hart tapped me on the shoulder. "I'll help whenever I can, Mrs. Malloy, and I'm sure Coach Finley will, too." Jerry nodded without enthusiasm.

In the front of the room, Mr. Weiss's expression turned to stone. "Coach Finley may find himself occupied with other matters, Miss Hart. I received certain information today from Farber College that may shed a new light on Coach Finley's career at our school."

That earned a collective gasp, followed by furtive looks and whispers. Sherwood murmured, "Has Weiss made a *lapsus lingua*, do you think?" His comment earned a kick from Evelyn. "A slip of the tongue," he translated in a wounded tone as he rubbed his shin.

Jerry stood up, his hands on his hips like a playground combatant. His blue eyes were circles of slate, his dimples tucked away for the moment. "What's that supposed to mean, Mr. Weiss?"

"That means, Mr. Assistant Coach Finley, that you and I shall have a long conversation as soon as the auditors are gone."

"As long as I have your attention, Mr. Weiss," Jerry continued tightly, "what about Immerman's eligibility? He said you refused to consider a temporary suspension of the rule until midsemester grades are in. That means he can't play in the Homecoming game. Our policy says that—"

"I am aware of our school policy. I do not need a first year assistant coach to explain it to me, nor do I care to engage in an argument about my decisions. Immerman is no longer eligible to participate in extracurricular activities, in that his grades are below one point two five. Is that clear?"

"As clear as mud, Mr. Weiss!" Our gray-clad hero stormed out of the room without a parting glance for Miss Hart, who seemed on the verge of a collapse. Beside me, Evelyn looked grim, but Sherwood Timmons was battling not to snicker too loudly. I considered a kick, but opted for a glower.

"*Dum spiro, spero,*" he said, shrugging. "While I breathe, I hope."

"Shut up, Sherwood," Evelyn hissed. She looked back at Paula Hart. "Don't worry about it, honey. Once the auditors arrive, Weiss will forget all about this. But in the meantime, keep Jerry away from him."

Paula's eyes filled with tears, but she bravely held them back. "Jerry doesn't deserve to be abused, and it's not fair," she said in true pioneer-woman fashion.

Miss Dort cleared her throat. "One final item, please! Today I noticed a marked increase in the flow of students in the hallways during class, especially from the basement. Any student who leaves your room for any reason must have a blue slip with the current date, room of origin, destination, and your signature. Is that clear?"

Oh, dear. How slipshod some teacher must be to allow students to roam the hallways without blue slips. I slumped down and stared at my ankles, which are trim and appealing. When those around me began to shuffle, I presumed it was safe and stood up.

Evelyn accompanied me to the sunless labyrinth of the basement. "By the way, Claire," she said as I turned toward the cave door, "on Fridays we have a potluck lunch in the lounge. The Furies, Paula and Jerry, the Latin pedant, and whoever else drops by. Sherwood considers it a prime opportunity to needle any and all of the aforementioned, but you mustn't pay any attention to him."

"I haven't yet," I said. "I understand from the gossip that he and Paula used to—to, ah . . ."

She laughed. "For almost three years, Sherwood had a jewel, and he knew it. She did his tax returns, balanced his personal checkbook and that of the Latin Club, edited and typed his manuscript, and did almost everything a devoted wife would do for her hubby. All in hopes, I'm afraid, that he would marry her so that she could quit teaching and start reproducing in a vine-covered cottage."

"Then Jerry showed up?" I said encouragingly. I will admit to a flicker of shame for encouraging gossip. A teensy flicker. Curiosity snuffed it.

"He strolled into the first staff meeting of the year in his saggy gray sweats, his blond hair flopping in his eyes and his boyish grin just a shade shy. Paula melted; she hasn't recovered since."

"Was Sherwood devastated by the loss of free labor?" I was now utterly shameless, and I scolded myself without mercy as I panted for further details.

"More irritated than devastated, I believe. He does sulk whenever the lovebirds coo too loudly in the lounge, but other than that, he seems to have recovered. He may think he can persuade me to take over her duties."

"Is that possible?" Pant, pant.

"As the kids would say, no way. I was married once upon a time, to a tool salesman from Toledo. During the first trimester of newly wedded bliss, I had the opportunity to meet two of his other wives. And I thought bigamy was reserved for Mormons!" Laughing, she waved and clicked away down the hall.

I picked up a bundle of old *Falcon Criers* and started for the stairs and a dose of scotch. As I passed the teachers lounge, I heard loud voices from its interior.

"Jerry," Paula said with surprising vehemence, "there's nothing he can do to you. Even if he does fire you, there are lots of coaching jobs in other schools. It'll be okay."

"He's a damn tyrant. How in the hell did he ever get hold of my transcript, anyway? I'm doing a good job with the team. Fred thinks I'm a good assistant coach, and so do the boys. We have a chance at the district title, Paula. Fred's talking about retiring at the end of the school year, which means I could take over the head coach position. We could afford to get married!"

"Oh, Jerry," she sighed.

Conversation halted. Anyone with an ounce of scrupulosity would have tiptoed away, and allowed the two to do whatever they were doing in private. I edged closer to the door.

Jerry came up for air. "Somebody ought to do something about Weiss. Maybe I'm the somebody."

"What can you do? He already knows about your past, and he's probably told Miss Dort. She'll tell the Furies, and they'll broadcast it to God." Paula was trying to sound stern and sensible.

"I'll think of something." Jerry merely sounded angry.

Wincing, I opted to retreat before the door opened and my nose was creased. I turned around and ran into Sherwood Timmons, who was wiggling his eyebrows like venetian blinds.

"Trouble in paradise?" he murmured, noticeably undistressed. "Could there be some bone of contention between the two?"

"I have no idea. I came by to see if I left a folder in the lounge."

"And were prevented ingress by our Echo and Narcissus? Did you catch them in *flagrante delicto*?"

Evelyn had the right idea—and the right shoes—to deal with Sherwood. I gave him a quick frown and went around the corner to go upstairs, but he followed like a faithful old dog. Or a slobbering old bloodhound. I gave up and stopped.

"Yes, Mr. Timmons? Was there something else?"

He backed me into a corner, close enough for me to smell a hint of wintergreen on his breath. "Would you be interested in a peek at the journalism accounts, Mrs. Malloy?"

We had found the darkest corner of the basement, which was no sunlit meadow to begin with. I dared not glance at the ceiling, due to a phobia of bats and other rabid creatures, including men in goatees.

I put a finger on his chest to remove him from my face. "Why would I be interested in a peek at the journalism accounts, Mr. Timmons? I'm a substitute teacher, not a CPA."

He leaned forward and propped an arm on the wall above me. "Ah, but in reality you are a bookseller—not a substitute teacher. It's rather obvious why you've come to Farberville High School, my dear literary peddler. Your reputation precedes you."

"What reputation might that be?"

"As our local amateur sleuth, dear woman. I'm sure all your activities were *pro bono publico*—"

"If you say one more syllable in Latin, I will yank off your goatee to use as a mascara brush. I will then apply my foot to your *gluteus maximus.*"

"My apologies; I shall do my utmost to restrain myself. Now, about your purpose for infiltrating our little school, Mrs. Malloy. May I call you Claire? It's obvious that you're on an undercover mission to expose the financial diddlings."

"It is? Perhaps I'm here to help out until a replacement can be found for Miss Parchester. Civic responsibility, a commitment to education of our youth, that sort of thing."

He chuckled at my silly attempt. "You're here to snoop around and discover our closet embezzler, Claire. You need not be ashamed. In truth, it's quite admirable. That's why I offered to help you get your lovely hands on the journalism accounts."

As a Mata Hari, I was not good. As a loser in the skirmish of wits, I could at least struggle for a graceful concession. "Where are the journalism ledgers? When I couldn't find them in the journalism room, I presumed Miss Dort locked them away in the office for the auditors."

Sherwood put a hand in his pocket and pulled out a key. "She did, but that needn't stop us. Shall we say tonight at midnight? The two of us, tiptoeing through the darkened hallways lit only by shafts of moonlight, our hearts pounding wildly yet in unison as we approach our shadowy destination?"

A door opened across the hall. Pitts smirked and said, "I'm supposed to fumigate the offices tonight, kids. Try a motel, or the backseat of a car." The door closed with a soft squeak.

"Do you think he heard the entire conversation?" I gulped.

Sherwood took my elbow to steer me up the stairs to the land of the living. "Pitts has an ear to every wall and a finger in every cesspool. Luckily, he is too much the resident troglodyte to use the information wisely."

"Well, we can't get into the office tonight," I said, relieved. My conscience (a.k.a. duty to Miss Parchester) prodded me to add, "I suppose we could try tomorrow night. Midnight seems overly furtive; shall we say ten o'clock?"

Sherwood agreed, although he looked vaguely disappointed by my more prosaic suggestion. In the parking lot, he hopped into a red sports car and roared away in a cloud of dust. I chugged home, left my purse on the living room floor, and headed for the nectar of the gods. And I don't mean apricot juice.

"F"O"U"R"

I felt obliged to appear the next day at dear old FHS. Miss Parchester had telephoned the previous evening; I had admitted failure and defeat, rather hoping she would tell me to forget the silly scheme. She had wished me luck.

The cave was hardly home sweet home, but the aroma was familiar. When the homeroom bell emptied the hall, I took my personalized coffee cup (I had scratched an *M* on the bottom, as in "mindless") to the lounge, left a box of saltines and a package of cream cheese in the refrigerator (I hate potlucks), and filled my cup (I need caffeine). All this was accomplished in semi-solitude. A mute Fury came and went, but the lounge lovebirds apparently had found another place to wish each other good morning.

I returned to the cave in time to greet the first class. They chattered, I read, and the bell rang. The second-period class came on schedule. I had just counted noses and settled them down when the door opened, and Miss Parchester tiptoed in. She wore a baggy blue coat, a plastic rain scarf, and galoshes. She had an umbrella in one hand, but it may have had more sinister applications than protection from the elements. For the record, the sky had been blue and cloudless when I went underground earlier.

"I thought I'd drop by to see if I might help you in any way," she murmured apologetically. "You mentioned that the Falconnaire would be published as scheduled. Perhaps I can offer a few words of advice."

"Ah, thank you, Miss Parchester," I said. "But are you sure you ought to be here? Mr. Weiss might be upset if he knew you. . . ."

She clasped her hands over her bosom as her eyes began to fill with tears. The umbrella swished past my nose with only an inch to spare. "I so wanted to visit, Mrs. Malloy, if only to see my dear students for a brief moment."

Her dear students were gaping like guppies, their eyes unblinking and their little mouths opening and closing silently. I took her elbow and escorted her into the darkroom. "I'm not sure this is wise, Miss Parchester. I appreciate your offer to help with the yearbook, but I don't want you to jeopardize the situation. It really might be better for you to slip away before anyone else notices you."

She gazed up at me. Her breath would have pickled a cucumber at one hundred feet, and her eyes were etched with fine red lines. I realized she had tied one on since breakfast, no doubt with her blessed mother and the Judge in attendance. Her sorrowful smile was interrupted by a hiccup.

"Oh, dear." She covered her mouth with her hand. "I must have sipped my tea too quickly in my haste to visit you."

"Oh, dear," I echoed weakly. "Let me bring you a cup of coffee from the lounge, Miss Parchester. Black coffee, I think."

She caught my arm in a birdlike claw. "I much prefer"— hic—"tea, dear. Coffee does stain one's dentures. You're much too young to worry about that, but we senior citizens must be careful."

I was aging rapidly; gray hairs were popping out each second I remained in the darkroom with the tipsy trespasser. "One cup of coffee won't do any permanent damage. Trust me. Now, if you'll promise to sit on this stool—"

"You're too kind," she said, shifting from manic to maudlin with amazing ease. "It's been so dreadful these last few days. Everyone must think I'm a common criminal, a petty thief with no conscience. I am beginning to wonder if I might have made an error—although I must assure you it was done in innocence. I—" She broke off with a helpless quiver.

"I'm sure any error was unintentional, Miss Parchester. Please let me bring you a cup of coffee. Please."

She shook her head as she dug through her purse for a handkerchief. We were seconds away from a deluge that was apt to result in a forty-day cruise. Black coffee, in quantity. Immediately. I opened the door, but again the claw stopped me.

"I shall go to the lounge on my way out of the building," she said. "I brought a jar of my brandied peach compote for Mr. Weiss. He is terribly fond of it, and I thought he might enjoy it even if—if—it was brought by a common thief!" She squared her shoulders, lifted her chin, gave me a jaunty wave, and weaved through the door. A hiccup sufficed for a farewell.

The guppies and I watched her coattail disappear around the corner. I frowned warningly, and they began to whisper among themselves. Miss Parchester's brief appearance would not remain a secret, nor would her condition. The peach compote was not the only thing with a slug of brandy in it.

Thirty minutes later the bell rang. I went down the hall to the teachers lounge, aware that I was apt to find Miss Parchester snoring on a sofa. The room was empty. I refilled my coffee cup and sat down on the mauve-and-green to think of a way to salvage the poor woman's reputation.

Evelyn came out of the ladies room. "That room is filthier every day. Pitts is impossible; I wish Weiss would do something about finding a replacement."

"Did you happen to see Miss Parchester in here earlier?" I waited to hear whether the woman in question was asleep in a stall in the ladies room—or worse.

"Oh, my God, is she in the building? Weiss will have a tantrum if he finds out. He's in a foul mood today, and——"

A thin young woman rushed into the lounge. She pulled a tissue from her pocket and began to wipe furiously at her dripping eyes. Small, muffled sobs came from under the tissue. I stared at the display of misery, unsure how to offer comfort or aid. Before I could decide, the woman crammed the tissue in her pocket and flew out the door.

"My student teacher," Evelyn explained. "She is no match for the French II class. They get her every day at about this time."

"And she wants to be a teacher?"

"When she grows up. I didn't see poor Miss Parchester, so we can hope she left before Weiss spotted her. Are you ready for our weekly potluck free-for-all?"

I admitted that my preparations had extended only to a stop at the grocery store on my way to school. A brief stop, at that.

Evelyn shook her finger at me. "The Furies live for the whoosh of the Tupperware containers on Friday, Claire. Our little luncheons are a major part of their social activities—those and chaperoning the school dances. What a life."

"I'm supposed to be chaperone!" I buried my face in my hands. "Miss Dort informed me that I was to appear in Miss Parchester's place. I tried to block it out."

"Don't worry about it. All you have to do is keep the kiddies sober and celibate, the band from undressing or eating their instruments, and the roof from collapsing. Don't forget earplugs— and shin guards, in case one of the sophomore boys asks you to dance."

"Asks me to dance? I trust you're making a little joke, Evelyn. I would no more dance with a sophomore boy than I would balance a desk on my nose while chanting the Koran."

"They make book on it in the boys' bathroom. I believe it's some sort of primitive rite of passage. I was worth ten dollars.

The Furies, on the other hand, run into larger sums, thus far unclaimed."

"I don't intend to be a substitute for more than a few days. Miss Dort is searching for a certified teacher to replace me. I may take out an ad in the *New York Times*." I sank back in the bilious plaid. "Tell me about the Furies, Evelyn. I can't seem to keep them straight."

"Only Bernice can do that. They are equally drab, tedious, and morally superior. They kept Paula in tears for months, but she finally learned to stand up to them or simply ignore them."

"Why are they so hard on her?"

"She has made two very serious breaches of conduct in the lounge. For one thing, she has committed the sin of being young and pretty. The girls all adore her, and the boys can barely breathe when she bends over someone's typewriter in the classroom. Her second sin is to encourage Jerry to come in the lounge."

"He's a teacher, isn't he? Why shouldn't he come in the lounge with the rest of us?"

"He is also a coach. Coaches do not come into the lounge; they loiter in their offices or on the fields. It's an unwritten law that coaches and principals avoid the lounge. Coaches are inclined to smell of physical exertion, and principals are the topic of many conversations. Weiss has been lurking in here since the beginning of the semester, mostly in order to glower at Jerry and Paula."

"I thought Sherwood—"

"Herbert Weiss is a notorious lecher, despite a vague presence known as Mrs. Herbert Weiss. She materializes each year for fifteen minutes at the faculty Christmas party, where she smiles politely at everyone, and then vanishes until the following December. I doubt she has any effect on her husband or daughter."

"Does every male in the building have his eye on Paula?" I asked. "It sounds ominously competitive."

"As far as I know, Weiss and Sherwood are the primary contenders for the maiden's hand. To their regret, it is not available for warm, suggestive squeezes."

The door opened before I could elicit any more details of the idle, but nevertheless interesting, gossip. Sherwood Timmons had a bottle of champagne in his hand.

"I thought we might celebrate the arrival of blessed Friday," he announced as he went into the kitchenette and put the bottle in the refrigerator. "What is this? Could Emily Parchester have been sneaking around the basement this very morning, brandied peach compote bulging in her purse?"

"She came by to see me," I called. I did not elaborate, but it wasn't necessary.

Sherwood stuck his head out the door with an impish grin. "I heard she was a bit *non compos mentis,* but her compote—*sic itur ad astra* . . . her pathway to the stars."

"If Pitts hasn't been pawing in it," Evelyn said. "I think we ought to use the lounge fund to buy a padlock for the refrigerator."

"That would merely delay him," Sherwood said. The refrigerator door closed, and water ran in the sink. "The man could pick it with his teeth if motivation were strong enough."

While I pondered the wisdom of a diet, the door opened again. The Furies stalked in and took places on a sofa across from me. Miss Dort came in seconds later and continued into the ladies room. Mr. Weiss was next, followed by Jerry and Paula Hart.

Large, black clouds rolled in from the hallway. Lightning crackled invisibly, and thunder crashed soundlessly. The air was thick with odorless ozone. What air there was. I wondered if they really went through this every Friday, and for what reason. Fun, it clearly wasn't.

Evelyn stood up. "Well, shall we eat?"

Herbert Weiss stared at Jerry, who returned the gaze with ill-disguised anger. Paula tugged at her coach's hand and whispered something in his ear, but he brushed her aside. Sherwood smiled to himself. The Furies wiggled on the sofa and tried to look uninterested.

"Shall we eat?" Evelyn repeated, a hostess to the bitter end. "Claire, will you help me bring things to the table?"

I strolled into the kitchenette where I had to grab a drawer handle to keep myself upright. "Why are we doing this?" I hissed. "This is not my idea of a gala party."

Evelyn shrugged and began to pull plastic bowls and boxes out of the refrigerator. She piled them in my arms, balanced a stack of napkins on top, and sent me into the lion's den. She followed with paper plates, the champagne, and someone's saltines.

With the high spirits of a funeral cortege, we assembled around the table. Jerry sat down next to Paula at one end; the Furies formed a row across one side, impenetrably grim. The rest of us scattered about to act as buffers. Plastic lids whooshed loudly in the silence.

Mrs. Platchett examined a tidy formation of deviled eggs. "I see no sign that Pitts has been foraging today. It is safe to eat."

"Alcoholic beverages are not permitted on campus," Weiss snarled, pointing at the offending bottle.

Sherwood gave him a disdainful smile. "Are we reduced to following petty rules, Mr. Weiss? I presumed we were all above such things, but if you wish to insist. . . ?"

"Do whatever you want, Timmons. Perhaps we can have a discussion about your manuscript one of these days, if you're not too busy doing research at the college library."

"*Ars longa, vita brevis,*" Sherwood snapped. It was menacing, in an obscure way. He did not offer a translation, and for once Evelyn did not prompt him to do so.

Weiss disappeared into the kitchenette. The soda machine rattled briefly, followed by a popping sound as a bottle was decapitated. He then called, "Has Miss Parchester been in the building,

Bernice? I told her quite firmly that she was not to come back until the auditors have completed their investigation."

"I'll telephone to remind her," Miss Dort said. She picked up her clipboard and scribbled a note.

The Furies looked as though they were on the edge of a rebuttal. Mrs. Platchett eyed the doorway with a frown, and on both sides of her her cohorts flared their nostrils and tightened their lips. Tessa Zuckerman (I thought) actually opened her mouth for a fleeting moment, then closed it with an unhappy sigh. Her complexion seemed excessively gray, as though she were inflated with fog.

Weiss came to the doorway with the jar of compote in his hand. He took a fork to pull out a dripping piece of yellow fruit, and with a greedy look, plopped it in his mouth. "I suppose I'll overlook her presence in the building this one time, since she did leave a little something for me. I may regret Miss Parchester's absence in the future; her compote is remarkable. Is there any way we might persuade her to share the recipe, Bernice?"

"I shall inquire when I speak to her." Miss Dort picked up the clipboard and scribbled yet another note.

"Exactly how much money is missing from the journalism account?" Sherwood asked, giving me a conspiratorial wink. "Enough for riotous living in some singles' condominium for silver-haired swingers?"

"The amount is hardly the issue, Timmons. The funds belong to the students, and the embezzlement is all the more serious because it threatens their trust," Weiss said through a mouthful of yellow goop. "In any case, I am aware of the gossip this situation has generated, and I want the entire faculty to put a stop to it. It is an administrative concern."

"I am confident Emily will be found innocent of any wrongdoing," Mrs. Platchett said. "Then the school can return to its normal routine, and the journalism students can once again have valuable experience in preparation for their careers. Emily quite inspires them, as you well know."

I sensed an aspersion on the substitute's ability to inspire said students. "We're working industriously on the yearbook," I said, taking a deviled egg with a devil-may-care look. "We hope to complete the sophomore layout next week." Whatever that was.

"But we have no newspaper over which to chuckle," Sherwood said. "I was finding the Miss Demeanor column quite compelling, if not exactly Pulitzer material. Just as it was becoming most interesting, it was cut off in its prime. Of course, *humanum est errare,* but in the Xanadu Motel? One wonders if something might be astir within our little community. . . ."

"The insinuation of a tawdry scandal is inappropriate for a school newspaper," Miss Dort sniffed. "Mr. Weiss and I both agree that impressionable adolescents should not be exposed to that sort of thing. As faculty advisor, Miss Parchester had an obligation to forbid the publication of such filth. She refused to comply with the numerous memos I sent regarding the situation, citing some nonsense about freedom of the press. This is a school, not a democracy; the students have whatever rights we choose to allow them."

Weiss gave her an approving smile as he shoveled in the last of the peach compote. The smile died suddenly. He clutched his abdomen and doubled up as the contents of his stomach disgorged on the carpet. His scalp turned red, his face white. "Bernice," he managed to croak. "My God! Help me!"

"Herbert? What's—what's the matter?" she answered, shoving back her chair to run across the room and clasp his arm. She looked wildly at us over his back. "Do something to help him! Get a doctor!"

"I don't need a doctor," Weiss said abruptly, his voice weak but more normal than it had been seconds ago. He yanked his arm free and stood up, a handkerchief already in hand to wipe his chin. "I'm fine now. I don't know what came over me, but I certainly will not permit it to happen again. Have Pitts get in here immediately, and call the carpet cleaning service to make— reservations."

"Reservations?" Miss Dort said. She picked up her clipboard and began to write in precise little scratches, although without her usual briskness. "Carpet service—reservations. Why don't you lie down on the sofa for a few minutes, Mr. Weiss? You look rather pale."

He nodded and stretched out on the mauve-and-green. Miss Dort left the lounge, presumably to fetch the despicable Pitts, and returned within a minute or two. The rest of us toyed with our lunches, our earlier enthusiasm dampened by the increasingly pervasive stench. Even the Furies seemed to find it difficult to pick up the cadence of sound nutritional practices.

"Damn doctors shouldn't be allowed to teach," Weiss said suddenly, his finger poking holes in the air. "Think they're too damn good for the rest of us."

"I'll make a note of it," Miss Dort said, her voice noncommital despite the bizarre words coming from the principal. She stared defiantly at us, daring us to offer an editorial. No one moved.

"Bunch of copycats," Weiss said. He jerked up and glared at us through wide, glazed eyes. Suddenly they bulged like balloons as he clasped his throat. Burbling wildly, he clawed the air. His hands froze, and he slowly rolled off the sofa to sprawl on the rug.

Miss Dort scrambled to her feet and shrieked something about an ambulance as she ran out of the lounge. Paula grabbed Jerry, while Sherwood and Evelyn went over to touch the unmoving shoulder with timid fingers. Mrs. Platchett clasped her bosom.

"Oh, my goodness," she announced whitely.

The Fury on her left sighed, but the third stole the show. "Oh, dear," she whooshed as she toppled out of her chair. The ensuing thud was fainter and more ladylike than the previous one, but it sounded painful and seemed to bring us out of our collective shock and into action, albeit chaotic and ineffectual.

Ambulance attendants dashed in a few minutes later. The fainted Fury was on a sofa, attended by her sisters. Mr. Weiss was still facedown on the stained carpet; there hadn't been much reason to worry about his comfort. The rest of us were standing about, wringing our hands both literally and figuratively, while muttering inanities about heart attacks and/or strokes. How sudden they were, etc.

Miss Dort came in behind the attendants, and behind her was the rabbity little man I'd seen in the main office.

"Oh, this is terrible!" he sputtered. "I just cannot believe—believe that—that this sort of tragedy—absolute tragedy—could—"

"Shut up, Chips," Miss Dort said absently, intent on the body on the floor. "What was it—a heart attack?"

One of the attendants stood up and studied us with a masked expression. "No, it wasn't a heart attack. You'd better call the police."

"Why?" Miss Dort countered. Her fingers tightened around the clipboard, which was pressed against her chest like a shield.

"The guy was poisoned, lady."

Miss Dort blanched, took a step backward, and slowly collapsed in the doorway. The clipboard clattered down beside her.

The room was beginning to resemble the forest scene after Mount St. Helen's eruption. I glared at the ambulance attendants. "I will call the police. In the meantime, why don't you occupy yourselves with the lady on the floor or the one on the sofa? You do have some paramedical training, don't you?"

Grumbling, they split up to deal with the supine figures. I went upstairs to the office, shoved past the pimply Cerberus, and snatched up the telephone. The number was familiar; seconds later Peter Rosen came on the line.

"So glad you called," he said with an audible smile. "There's a wonderfully terrible movie at the drive-in theater, something about a giant asparagus attacking a major metropolitan area. We may end up parked beside your students, but I thought it—"

I interrupted and told him what had happened. He then interrupted and told me that he and his squad would be there shortly. I tried to interrupt with a question or two, but it didn't work. I was speaking to a dial tone.

A keen-eared secretary came out of her room to goggle at me. I told her to announce on the intercom that all students should go to fourth-period classrooms and remain there until further notice, and told her which teachers would have to wait in the lounge for the CID. She nodded, I shrugged, and we both marched off to our respective duties.

Miss Dort and the Fury were still unconscious, but everyone else looked fairly chipper. Evelyn and Sherwood huddled in one corner, watching the attendants wave vials under noses. Jerry and Paula cuddled in a second corner to whisper. The two conscious Furies hovered about, pale but determined, although I wasn't at all sure what they were determined to do.

Mr. Weiss hadn't produced any motion that I could see. I muttered something about the police being on the way, then perched on an arm of a mustard-and-red sofa. When the door opened, I assumed that Peter and his minions had broken all speed records to rescue me. How wrong I was.

Pitts slithered in, a bucket in one hand and a mop in the other. His reptilian eyes were bright. "Well, I'll be a bullfrog's bottom. I heard that Weiss had dropped dead in the lounge, but I didn't think it was true. I'll be a bullfrog's bottom on a hot summer night!"

From her corner, Evelyn snapped, "Get out of here, Pitts! Go mop a hallway or something."

He scratched his head with the mop handle. "What'd he kick off from? And what's wrong with them two?"

Peter came in before Pitts could suffer the same fate of the soda bottle—decapitation. He glanced at me, then began to order everyone about with cold authority. Miss Dort was revived in time to accompany the group to a vacant classroom next to the lounge; the Fury refused to cooperate and was rolled away on a gurney. She looked extremely ill.

Then we sat. A bell rang, but no footsteps tromped down the hall. I told Miss Dort what I had arranged with the secretary, and was rewarded with a pinched frown. It had seemed quite efficient to me. I hadn't even had a clipboard.

Sherwood wiggled his eyebrows at me, no doubt intending to look conspiratorial. "So our *summum bonum* was poisoned. Have you identified the murderer, Claire, or are you waiting for a more propitious moment for a denouement?"

Before I could respond, Paula Hart stumbled to her feet and dashed out of the room. A uniformed officer returned her without comment, and she sank down in a desk to sniffle bravely. Jerry went over to pat her shoulder.

Sherwood murmured, "I'm surprised you have tears for such things, my dear. After all, Weiss was about to dismiss and disgrace your beloved, which would have complicated the daily allotment of stolen kisses in the lounge. Now, you and your *particeps criminis* are free to indulge yourselves."

Jerry growled. "Look, Timmons, Paula and I had nothing to do with this. Weiss and I might have had hard feelings, but I sure as hell didn't poison him."

We all exchanged uneasy looks.

Sherwood clapped his hands with the glee of an infant beholding a popsicle. "The brandied peach compote! How utterly fascinating! Miss Parchester has more strength of character than I had credited her with."

Now Evelyn, Miss Dort, Paula, Jerry, and the two Furies all growled, sounding like a pack of wild dogs converging on a wounded animal. Sherwood smiled at them, but his goatee trembled and his eyes flickered in my direction.

Pitts, who had managed to include himself in the group, chortled. "I saw that yellow slime on the floor. Is that what killed the old man? Miss Parchester was here earlier; I saw her sneak into the lounge, and she had a funny look on her puss."

She probably did look rather peculiar, but I saw no point in discussing her condition with the lizard. "Mr. Pitts," I said, "you were not a witness to the unpleasantness in the lounge, so there really is no reason for you to be here. I'll speak to Lieutenant Rosen about allowing you to leave." For Mongolia, on a train.

"I saw plenty of interesting stuff. I know who went in the lounge—and why. Mr. Fancy Lieutenant Rosen will be pretty damn eager to talk to me."

Mr. Fancy himself came into the classroom. "We have not finished with the lounge. I'll need a room from which to conduct my investigation."

Miss Dort fluttered her clipboard. "I'll see to it at once, Lieutenant. However, what shall I do about the students and other faculty? The bus schedule will require modification, and—"

"Don't do anything," Peter said hastily. "Is there someone who can take charge upstairs for the remainder of the school day?"

"Mr. Chippendale is the dean, but I doubt he could manage," Miss Dort said, shaking her head. "And who will notify Mrs. Weiss and poor little Cheryl Anne?"

Peter beckoned to the officer in the doorway, and told him to locate Mr. Chippendale. Paula Hart mentioned that Cheryl Anne was in the typing room at the end of the hall and left to tell her the news before the gossip spread. Once bureaucratic details were under control, Peter gazed around the room at his collection of witnesses.

"Cyanide, I think," he said conversationally, as though running through the menu for a dinner party, "although we'll have to run tests to be sure. I would guess it was introduced in that yellowish substance on the floor. Would anyone care to tell me where it came from?"

We all stared at the floor. The linoleum hadn't seen a mop in at least a decade.

Pitts waggled his mop. "I can tell you exactly where the goop came from, sir. Miss Emily Parchester brought a jar of brandied peach compote this morning, 'cause she knows how much Weiss liked it. I think you got yourself a murderer, sir."

Peter looked at me. "Is that true, Mrs. Malloy?"

Presumably I was the very same Mrs. Malloy with whom he shared bottles of wine and moments of ecstasy on an occasional basis. He seemed to have forgotten. I stared at him and said, "She did leave a jar of compote in the kitchenette, but she did not lace it with cyanide, Lieutenant."

"That will have to be determined," he said. He paused as a gurney squeaked past the closed door on its journey to the morgue. "I'll need to take statements from each of you. Will Miss Parchester's address and telephone number be available in the main office?"

Mrs. Platchett rose like a missile head. "Emily Parchester did not leave a jar of poisoned compote in the lounge, Lieutenant. Her father was Judge Amos Parchester of the state Supreme Court, and her mother came from a very old Farberville family."

"The Borgias were an old family, too," Sherwood commented. "That hardly kept the children from——"

"Who are you?" Peter said. His teeth glinted, wolf-style. His molasses-colored eyes were flecked with yellow flints.

I might have melted, but Sherwood merely bobbed his head. "Sherwood Timmons, at your service. I was speaking in jest; *nemine contradicente* when I say that we all have faith in Miss Parchester's unflagging innocence."

Evelyn once again overlooked his verbal transgression. "Emily is hardly the sort to do such a thing, Lieutenant. She's a harmless old lady who taught journalism for forty years, until unfortunate circumstances forced her to retire."

"The journalism teacher," Peter said. He turned back to me. "She was here earlier today, with the compote. Weiss was fond of the stuff."

"The jar was left in the kitchenette for over half an hour," I retorted. "Anyone could have put cyanide in it."

"But why?" he countered.

I tried not to glance at Jerry, who had been thundering threats the previous afternoon, or at Sherwood, who might have been muttering them in Latin. "I have no idea, Lieutenant Rosen."

Paula Hart had been there, too. "Jerry didn't mean what he said," she offered tremulously. She clutched his hand and held it to her cheek as she stared defiantly at Peter.

"What didn't he mean?"

"He was only kidding when he said someone ought to take care of Mr. Weiss," she said. The girl was a veritable wealth of helpful information. "Jerry didn't poison the compote."

The coach's face matched his gray sweats. "That's right, Lieutenant, I was just blowing off steam."

Peter was unmoved by the sincerity glowing on the young faces. "Let's discuss it in private," he suggested with a smile. His teeth—or should I say fangs—glistened in the subsequent silence.

From the *Falcon Crier,* October 29

Dear Miss Demeanor,
   Do you think it's undignified for juniors to throw eggs and toilet paper at houses on Halloween and basically act like children? I think it's immature, gross and utterly disgusting.

Dear Reader,
   Miss Demeanor senses an underlying trepidation in your letter.

She wonders if you're worried that no one will throw an egg at you or decorate your lawn with white steamers. Have no fear: Miss Demeanor has your address.

Dear Miss Demeanor,
  I'm a sophomore with a terrible problem. You see, this boy wants me to go steady, but we both have braces. I read somewhere that the braces can get locked. I would absolutely die if that happened.

Dear Reader,
  Miss Demeanor wonders where in the annals of history going steady got locked with kissing. Sophomores have no business kissing, anyway. Take advantage of your lowly status to perfect hand-shaking and meaningful looks. Then, Miss Demeanor suggests that you search for a boy whose father is an orthodontist, for financial as well as utilitarian concerns.

Dear Miss Demeanor,
  How's this for a trick-or-treat surprise? I call somebody's wife and tell her that her husband has a standing reservation at the Xanadu Motel every Thursday afternoon. Do you think she'd get a kick out of that?

Dear Reader,
  Although Miss Demeanor promised to answer every letter in her box, she must admit this motel business is becoming a bit tedious. This is clearly adult stuff. The only person who's getting a kick out of it is you, Reader. If you call somebody's wife, you're likely to get another kick—in the rear. Can we just drop it, please?

"F"I"V"E"

The afternoon did not skip by; it trudged in lead-lined snow-shoes. At the end of the last period, the students were sent away. Several hundred of them found a reason to parade down the basement hallway, all very casual and distracted by meaningful inner dialogue. Adolescents respond to violence much the same way moths do to a candle, or iron filings to a magnet. It is not endearing.

We were not sent away. Peter set up shop in the lounge at the formica table, and each of us was called in to make a statement. My name was the last on his list, which fooled me not at all, and it was almost four o'clock before I was beckoned into his parlor.

I glanced at the chalked silhouette on the carpet and the circular stain of dampness. "Did you arrive at any brilliant deductions in the last four hours? I would have offered suggestions, but I was having too much fun in that dusty room counting flowers on the wall and cracks in the ceiling."

He grinned at me. His curly black hair and three-piece suit gave him the appearance of either an executive or a Mafia hit man. He's clearly a New Yorker, from the jutting nose to the jarring accent, but I had grown accustomed to his face, among other things. He has talents that are best left unspecified. At the moment, we were lovers, although it was much like making goulash with dynamite and nitroglycerine. Too much personality, and usually not in tune. However, we did certain things very well, and legal entwining was occasionally discussed. I was the one who shied away. I have tried marriage; the results were not distasteful, but I have learned to enjoy my unwedded solitude.

"I deduced," Peter said wryly, "that this place rivals any afternoon soap opera for intrigues, gossip, and back-stabbing, to put it mildly. Do these people actually teach?"

"It does boggle the mind, doesn't it?" I said, sitting on the mauve-and-green monster. "I've felt as if I had been airlifted into Peyton Place the last two days. What have you learned thus far?"

"This is an official investigation, Claire," he said. The grin inverted itself into a frown. "I know that you haven't paid any attention to that niggling little detail in the past, but this time I want you to stay out of it."

"As long as Miss Parchester is out of it," I said with a lofty expression. It never failed to irritate him.

"Emily Parchester is very much in it, for the moment. She did sneak into the building with a jar of peach compote, knowing that Weiss was especially fond of it. She, on the other hand, was not at all fond of him. The compote was laced with cyanide, possibly from inception. It's not easy to overlook the coincidence, Claire."

"It seems fairly easy to jump to conclusions, however. If you'd ever met her, you'd realize she's a harmless little old lady, not some character out of *Arsenic and Old Lace*. She's going to paint watercolors and ride in buses when she retires, for God's sake."

"Let's hope she hasn't already climbed aboard, then, since we don't seem able to find her. The uniformed officers have questioned her neighbors, but no one claims to have seen her since yesterday evening, when she discretely put a sack of liquor bottles in a garbage can. A large sack. We would very much like to discuss her recipe for peach compote."

"The entire Farberville police force can't find one old lady?" I laughed merrily. "Perhaps she's gone underground to escape the dragnet." I watch old shows on television when I can't sleep.

Very old shows, I suspect, since all the characters are either black, white, or gray.

"We'll find her," he said, unamused by my cleverness. "We should have a report from the medical examiner's office within twenty-four hours, but we're operating on the premise that the poison was in the damned yellow goop. It reeked of bitter almonds, as did Weiss's mouth. The symptoms were consistent with cyanide poisoning: nausea, cramps, mental confusion, and death within minutes. It's a painful poison, but it is reasonably easy to get one's hands on . . . and inexpensive for someone on a tight budget."

"You don't need to question her—just hook her up to the electric chair and throw the switch! You obviously think she's the culprit, simply because she brought the compote to school. It was sitting in the kitchenette for half an hour. Anyone could have added the cyanide."

"That's what *we'll* investigate. Now, I need a full statement from you so that we can get out of this place before dark."

A minion named Jorgeson appeared to write down my words of wisdom. I reiterated my movements for the last two days, from homeroom to sixth period. Without a whimper, I might add. Jorgeson rewarded my conciseness with a smile, I signed the silly thing, and we left the building together.

Always a gentleman, Peter walked me to my car. "I guess I can't take you to see *The Massachusetts Asparagus Massacre* at the drive-in tonight. After a break for hamburgers, we're going to search the entire building for anything with cyanide in it. I suspect we'll still be there when the homeroom bell rings Monday morning."

"I presumed you'd be on a stakeout at Miss Parchester's house." I gazed up with a sweet smile. "*Carpe diem,* Peter."

I drove out of the parking lot in a skimpy mist of dust, since I valued my shocks more than my desire for a grand exit. When I arrived home, I found Caron and Inez on the sofa, salivating for details.

"Oh, Mother," Caron sighed, "were you really there at the Fateful Moment? Did he clutch his throat and accuse Miss Parchester?"

Inez clutched her throat. "My sister was in Typing II when Miss Hart came in to break the ghastly news to Cheryl Anne. It was awful, Mrs. Malloy. Cheryl Anne turned white. Miss Hart was white, too, and crying, then all the girls started crying. None of them could finish the time test. Cheryl Anne had to go to the nurse's office to lie down."

"Did they find Miss Parchester?" Caron demanded. "Did she admit that she nursed a Secret Hatred of Mr. Weiss?"

"Did the police really discover her cowering in the basement?" whispered Inez.

I considered ignoring Tweedledee and Tweedledum, and taking a cup of tea to bed. On the other hand, the two were apt to be better informed than I; FHS was not a monastery, as I well knew. It was a radio station, complete with news bulletins and in-depth commentaries.

Once I was armed with tea, I returned to the living room. "So the popular theory is that Miss Parchester did it?"

Caron shook her head. "That's what the seniors think. The juniors think Coach Finley did it Out of Love, the sophomores are backing Mr. Timmons, and the——" She broke off with a funny expression. She has a variety of them, but this one was unfamiliar.

"And?" I prompted. I took a long drink, just in case.

Inez shot me her version of a funny expression. It was noticeably baleful, but tempered with sympathy—for Caron. "Some of the freshmen think you did it, Mrs. Malloy. Caron and I told them in no uncertain terms that you didn't, of course."

"Thank you, Inez. Why do the freshmen harbor such ideas?"

"Because you were so upset about the Falconnaire. Everybody

heard that you were livid in the teachers meeting, and snarled all sorts of threats at Mr. Weiss."

"And then poisoned him to avoid having to supervise work on the yearbook? Don't the freshmen find that a bit extreme?" I told myself that the question was absurd; I knew from personal experience that freshmen did indeed find things a bit extreme, including such things as life.

Caron sniffed. "Inez and I tried to tell them, Mother. I mean, the idea is preposterous. If the police will just find Miss Parchester, they can make her confess and clear your name." Not to mention other people who were saddled with the same name through no fault of their own.

The telephone rang. I went to answer it while I toyed with my defense. To my astonishment, Miss Emily Parchester was on the line.

"Mrs. Malloy, I was hoping you might be able to visit me sometime in the next day or two. I am quite curious about your progress in the mysterious case."

Mysterious was a mild description. I turned my back on the audience on the sofa and whispered, "Where are you?"

"I am at a country establishment, taking a rest for a few days while I try to keep this troublesome situation from disturbing me. I have experienced some difficulty in sleeping, and felt fresh air and the presence of a well-trained staff might soothe me. Have you made any progress?"

Nothing beyond being the freshman class's candidate for murderer, I thought bleakly. "There have been a few developments. Have the police not contacted you to discuss them?"

"Then the auditors are certain I was remiss in my accounts? Oh, Mrs. Malloy, whatever shall I do? The Judge must be rolling—"

"In his grave, on a rotisserie. Where is this establishment, Miss Parchester? I do think I'll come by for a visit today. Immediately."

She gave me directions, and I hung up. Caron and Inez were both flipping through magazines, competing for the title of Miss Nonchalance. I wondered what Caron found so fascinating in *Bookseller's Monthly Digest,* but I didn't ask. Instead, I said, "I'm going out for an hour or so, girls. Can you feed yourselves without burning down the kitchen?"

"Who was that on the telephone, Mother?"

"My Avon lady. The winter mascara has just arrived, and it may be my color. I'll see you later."

"What shall I tell Peter if he calls?" she continued, her lips pursed in great innocence as she adjusted an invisible halo.

"Tell him that I'll test 'Tarnished Copper' first."

Miss Parchester's so-called establishment was several miles out of town. The name was vaguely familiar, and I recalled its reputation when I stopped in front of a ten-foot-high iron gate. A chain-link fence topped with concertina wire disappeared into the woods in both directions, creating a formidable enclave designed to keep out hikers and stray dogs. Happy Meadows Home was not an ordinary country inn; it catered not to vacationers, but to inmates.

A guard appeared at my window, his eyes hidden behind reflective sunglasses. "You got business here?"

I checked my lipstick in the twin reflections. "I have come to see Miss Emily Parchester."

"You got permission from the office?"

"I was not aware I needed permission from the office," I said, mimicking his surly tone. "Is this a prison, and is Miss Parchester locked away somewhere in solitary confinement? For that matter, where are the happy meadows—and your supervisor?"

"I'll have to call the office, lady. No one's supposed to go in unless they got business." He went into a gatehouse and reappeared after several minutes. "You can talk to her medical advisor, but before you go in, I'll have to search your car and your person."

"Don't be silly," I said as I rolled up the car window. When the gate remained closed, I gave up and allowed the officious goon to search my car and purse, although I rebelled when he made a move toward my person. It has never been searched thus far—at least not for weapons or whatever he feared I had stashed under my unmentionables.

He ran a professional eye over my body, shrugged, and unlocked the gate. Wishing I had concealed a submachine gun on my person, I drove along a winding road to the front of a stately white house. No bars that I could see, but the goon at the gate did discourage trespassers. Once inside, I stopped at the reception desk and asked for Miss Parchester's room number.

I ended up in a claustrophobic room with a pale young man in a white coat. All he lacked was an oversized net and a hunchbacked, lisping lab assistant. "You wish to see Emily Parchester? This is highly irregular. Are you a family member or merely a friend?"

"I'm her attorney. She called me to discuss matters that are confidential." When he paled further, I went for the jugular. "The matters concern her incarceration in a certain establishment."

"Her stay is voluntary."

"That remains to be determined, perhaps through the auspices of our legal system. Now, if I may see my client. . . ?"

I was told that she was on the terrace, having tea. Feeling like a red-haired Joyce Davenport, I sailed out of the room and minutes later found myself with a porcelain teacup in one hand and a mushy cucumber sandwich in the other.

Miss Parchester beamed at me. "I am absolutely thrilled by your little visit, Mrs. Malloy. Although this establishment is restful, it does get a teeny bit boring. Now, what can I do to assist your investigation?"

"I still haven't found the accounts," I told her, suddenly remembering my appointment for that evening with Sherwood Timmons. It was out of the question now; I hoped he would realize the police might notice the two of us creeping down the hall. "Things are rather complicated at the moment, and I don't know when I'll be able to try to analyze the deposit slips."

"I'm sure you'll do your best. You're so kind to take on this burden for me; I don't know what I'd do without you. I've been so fortunate."

Without me, she wouldn't have visited the journalism room and dropped off her little gift in the lounge. She wouldn't have been accused of murder. She wouldn't have a policeman in the bushes beside her house or a supercilious lieutenant determined to arrest her at the first opportunity. I decided not to tell her how fortunate she was until I had cleared her name, along with the Judge's and dear mamma's.

"You're more than welcome," I murmured. "I was curious about the brandied peach compote, Miss Parchester. Did you use your normal recipe?"

"I used Aunt Eulalie's recipe, dear. It's been in the family for years and years. The Judge always spoke highly of it."

"And you didn't add anything to it?" I continued, inwardly wincing at the necessity of grilling an old lady, even if it was for her own good.

"No, I followed the recipe religiously." The faded blue eyes narrowed. "Was there something wrong with it? A funny taste or peculiar odor? The peaches were a few days old, and of course they're not as fresh as they were when one bought them directly from the farmer who came to the house in his wagon, but——"

I interrupted to tell her as gently as I could about the lethal consequences of the compote. Her teacup shattered on the flag-

stone surface as she turned ashen. A cucumber sandwich fell un-
noticed in her lap, and then tumbled onto her fuzzy pink slipper.

"Surely you speak in jest, Mrs. Malloy! I've made hundreds of
gallons of my special peach compote in my life, and no one has
ever accused me—accused me of—of poisoning—murdering
someone with—with—oh, dear!"

She stood up, looking frail and ill. The cucumber sandwich
was smashed to a white circle as she fled inside, leaving me alone
on the terrace.

I popped the last bite of sandwich in my mouth and started for my
car. A grim matron stopped me at the front door.

"You're the one who upset us, aren't you? Who are you and what
did you say to us? We're beyond coherence, and I cannot get a word
out of us. We are likely to have a relapse at any moment, just when
we're beginning to become nicely dried out and calm."

"I told us that a certain police detective thought we might
have poisoned our boss with peach compote," I explained politely. "If we have any sense at all, we'll keep us out of sight until
this thing is cleared up. We hope that we won't have to tell
anyone that we're at Happy Meadows, but we have a low pain
threshold, and they may force us to talk."

I left her to ponder the pronouns and went to my car. When I
arrived at home, it was blessedly still. I learned from a scrawled
note that Caron and Inez had gone out, destination unspecified. I
heated a Lean Cuisine, painted my toenails, ate, and tried to
watch television, which wasn't easy under the best of circumstances. I was staring at a blank screen when the doorbell rang.

Peter came in, his face lined with fatigue. I gave him a glass of
wine and sat down beside him. "Did we—I mean you, find any
cyanide in the building?"

"We found cyanide compounds in the journalism darkroom, in
the custodian's supply closet, in the secretary's desk to kill
roaches, and in both the biology and chemistry labs. We also

found a jar of rat poison in the girls' locker room and another in the band room. And another in the art room."

"Lots of cyanide."

"There is enough cyanide in the high school to kill off the entire student body and most of Farberville," Peter said, sighing. "We still have a few other rooms to search, and we'll probably find an adequate supply for the state. I thought poisons were supposed to be kept away from children."

"I'm very sorry the murderer didn't use some obscure South American tree sap." I toyed with an errant curl above his ear. It never failed to distract him, and I wanted to ease him in to a more pliable frame of mind. "Have you found Miss Parchester yet?"

"No, she hasn't come home. One of the neighbors saw her leave in a van, but had no idea what kind of van it was. We have an officer waiting at her apartment."

I tucked my feet under me and tried to look mildly sympathetic, as opposed to extremely curious. I did not ask if the van driver had reflective lenses and the warmth of a drill sergeant. "Did you learn anything of interest in the statements?"

"With a few exceptions, everyone seemed eager to assist us. Now I am well-informed of the bell schedule and the morning class times, the procedure with blue slips, the absentee reports, the alternate bus routes on snow days, and I know more than anyone should about computerized personal grade records. I also heard about Miss Parchester's little problem with the journalism accounts."

"All a misunderstanding."

"Isn't it interesting how you were available to substitute in the midst of the crisis? One would almost be inclined to think that your presence was along the lines of calling in the Mounties. . . ."

"As a member of the community and a concerned parent, I was merely helping out by agreeing to substitute," I said. Lied, actually—but only because he was looking so damned smug. "The students must have supervision. The perpetuity of the physical structure demands it."

"And you weren't trying to delve into the accounts?"

Ah, the burden of a reputation for brilliant deduction. I considered my next move as I refilled our wine glasses. I opted to delve into his accounts—of the crime.

"Miss Parchester left the journalism room at ten o'clock, and presumably put the jar in the refrigerator in the lounge," I commented in a conversational tone. "The jar was unattended for the next half hour, until I arrived. After that, no one came into the lounge."

"That's the time period we're interested in," Peter said. "The French teacher—ah, Evelyn West, said that she went into the lounge toward the end of second period for a cup of coffee. She saw the jar in the refrigerator, but did not realize that it was the infamous compote until later. That was at ten-fifteen or so."

"She didn't see anyone while she was there?"

"Her student teacher came in for a few seconds, but did not enter the kitchenette. Apparently, she comes in to cry on a regular basis." He gave me a puzzled look. "Does that make sense to you?"

"No, but I've witnessed it. Who else came to the lounge?"

"Bernice Dort, the vice-principal, came by for a soda, and our victim came in with her. Mrs. West says that they were unaware of her presence in the ladies room, but refused to elaborate. Miss Dort confirms the time."

"No one else came into the lounge?"

"According to the statements, no. You arrived at the beginning of the third period at about ten-thirty, right? You and Mrs. West were there until everyone arrived for the potluck, and no one else could have slipped into the kitchen to spike the compote."

I wrinkled my nose and tried to remember. "I think that's accurate," I admitted. "But what about the period from ten to ten-fifteen? Was anyone in the lounge then?"

Peter downed the last drop of wine and stood up. "No one has admitted being there, except for the custodian, who says he came in to clean the rest rooms."

"And he has cyanide in his closet! Pitts is the murderer, Peter;

I'm sure of it! He's the slimiest specimen of reptile I've ever seen, and he slinks around the building like a mongrel."

"But he doesn't have a motive."

"Yes, he does. Weiss was getting static from the teachers in the basement. Pitts hasn't been cleaning the classrooms for quite some time, and the teachers were beginning to get tired of the dirt. I know Miss Platchett was in Weiss's office earlier to demand that Pitts be terminated, preferably with extreme prejudice."

"That's not much of a motive," he pointed out. "Did Weiss agree to fire him?"

"It didn't sound like it, from the report I overheard. But that doesn't mean that Pitts might not be eager to prevent Weiss from taking drastic measures at a later date."

"By poisoning all the teachers in the lounge?"

"Maybe not. Miss Parchester wouldn't have risked it, either. Her dearest friends and staunchest supporters were likely to nibble the compote. She's hardly a Borgia sort."

I earned a gaze that blew straight from the North Pole. "I wouldn't know," he murmured, "since I haven't been able to locate the woman for a statement. No one seems to know where she is. Her friends don't know, her neighbors don't know, and her brother in Boise, Idaho, doesn't know."

"Well, don't look at me." Not like that, anyway. "You'd best run along and let me do some work on the yearbook layout. We teachers are a dedicated lot."

"As much as I'd like to stay and discuss the whereabouts of the elusive Miss Parchester, I wouldn't want to interfere with your obvious dedication. I'm going back to the high school to see if Jorgeson has found another gallon or two of cynaide in the home-economics room."

We parted amiably, if a shade warily. Corpses have always had that effect on our relationship.

"S"I"X"

Nothing much happened over the weekend. Peter called Sunday evening to say the CID was making little progress, but they had confiscated enough poison from the school to wipe out the country, if not the continent. The lab results were not yet in, so they had no theories as to the origin and composition of the cyanide compound. All of the teachers and staff had been questioned again, as had a few students who admitted they'd been in the halls during the second period. I mentioned that I hadn't been questioned again and was informed that I was not a suspect—or a particularly important witness. What charm the man possessed. The freshman class took me more seriously than he did, even if they overestimated the depth of my desire to avoid the yearbook.

Peter was not especially amused when I asked if he had found Miss Parchester, and his response does not bear repeating. Nor does mine when he inquired about my progress on the layout. The conversation ended on a slightly testy note when he reiterated his order about interference in the official investigation and I laughed. The man requires deflation to keep his head from exploding. It falls in the category of public service.

His little jibe did, however, remind me of earlier questions about the school newspaper's most infamous columnist. Said columnist was doing homework on her bed, a bag of potato chips within reach should malnutrition threaten to impair her intellectual skills. The radio blared in one ear, and the telephone receiver was affixed to the other.

I suggested she turn off, hang up, and cease stuffing potato chips in her mouth. After a nominal amount of dissension, we achieved an ambiance more conducive to conversation, albeit temporary and at great personal sacrifice on one party's part.

"When did you take over the Miss Demeanor column?" I asked.

"Last week. That's what makes all this So Irritating, Mother. If you don't do something about this mess, I'll never get to actually write the column. Bambi said—"

"So you didn't write any of the previous columns?"

"I intended to do the next one, but then Miss Parchester Absolutely Ruined Things by getting herself accused of embezzlement. This whole mess is incredible." And her mother's fault, although the sentiment remained unspoken.

"I'm sure Mr. Weiss agreed with you, as do his widow and daughter."

"I wouldn't be too sure about Cheryl Anne," Caron sniffed. "She hated her father because of what he did to Thud. Inez's sister said that Thud told one of the junior varsity linebackers that he wished he could meet Weiss in a dark alley some night."

"Does this have something to do with eligibility?" I remembered the discussion in the teachers' meeting, but not with any clarity. It hadn't made much sense.

"Thud's furious," Caron said solemnly. "So is Cheryl Anne. In fact, she's reputedly livid."

"What precisely is he ineligible to do? Produce an intelligible remark? Walk and count at the same time? Marry Cheryl Anne?"

Her expression resembled that of a martyr facing slings and arrows from a herd of drooling tribesmen. "Football, Mother. Thud is a big football jock, the captain of the team and all that, and plans to get a college scholarship for next year. Mr. Weiss pulled his eligibility, which means he won't get to play in the Homecoming game."

"Merely because he's flunking all his classes? How unkind of Mr. Weiss. After all, what's a mere education when it interferes with football?"

"It's our Homecoming game, Mother. If Starley City wins, it will be too humiliating for words. The dance will be a wake. Cheryl Anne is this year's Homecoming queen—naturally—and she's told everyone she'll literally die if the team loses on the most important night of her life." She eyed the telephone. "I really do need to work on my algebra. Big test on Wednesday."

"Your devotion to your education is admirable, but it will have to wait another minute or two. Has anyone suggested that Cheryl Anne or Thud might have—done something drastic because of the ineligibility problem and the impending ruination of Cheryl Anne's life?"

"It sounds rather farfetched, Mother, but I could call Inez and ask her if her sister's heard anything," Caron said with a flicker of enthusiasm. "Inez's sister hears Absolutely Everything. She's a cheerleader."

Caron was right; it did seem farfetched to poison daddy to ensure a football victory and subsequent festive celebration. Daddy's demise wouldn't guarantee that the eligibility would be reinstated, nor would Thud's presence on the field guarantee a victory. Neither of the two had access to the lounge, although it seemed as if cyanide in some form or other was accessible to all. I put the theory (which wasn't much good, anyway) aside and went on to a more promising line before my daughter commenced a full-scale rebellion.

"I need to speak to the girl who wrote the column before she caught mononucleosis," I said, raising one eyebrow sternly in case she made a grab for the telephone.

Caron produced the information. I razed her dreams by telling

her to stay off the telephone until I was finished, then ducked out
the door before her lower lip could extend far enough to endan-
ger me.

Rosie's mother was reluctant to allow me to speak to her, but
I finally persuaded her that I was not a girlfriend with a weekly
gossip report. Rosie came on the line with a timid, "Yes?"

I gave her a hasty explanation of my current position at the
high school, then asked how she chose the letters to answer in
her column.

"There's a box in the main office," she told me. "I emptied
the box every week and answered all the letters. I made a pledge
in the first issue, so it was vital to my journalistic integrity."

I had rather hoped Caron would mellow with age, but it
seemed we might have a few more years of tribulation if this was
the norm. "I found your column very amusing, Rosie. Some of it
rather puzzled me, though. What did you think about the
Xanadu Motel letters?"

"I thought somebody was bonkers, but I felt obligated to answer as best I could. It was vital to my—"

"Of course it was," I said quickly. "Did you have any idea
who wrote those letters? Any clues from the handwriting?"

"The letters were confidential, Mrs. Malloy," she said, sounding scandalized. "Even if I had been able to guess the identity of
the correspondents, I would never divulge the names. That would
compromise my—"

"Indeed," I said. I wished her a speedy recovery and a good
night's rest, then retreated to my bedroom. There wasn't any
reason to link the peculiar letters in the *Falcon Crier* with Weiss's
murder, or even with the accusations against Miss Parchester. It
was just a nagging detail, a petty and obscure campaign being
waged by an anonymous general against an equally anonymous
enemy. Who, according to the letters, spent many a Thursday
afternoon at the Xanadu indulging in activities that required little
speculation. After a few minutes of idle thought, I dismissed it

and spent the rest of the night dreaming of bell schedules, lounge visitors armed with lethal jars, and the prevalence of Tupperware.

Monday morning arrived. I arrived at dear old FHS and scurried down to the cavern just as the bell shrieked its warning to dilatory debutantes and lingering lockerites. As I stepped through the door, the intercom box crackled to life for the daily homeroom announcements. Miss Dort rattled off a brief acknowledgment of our beloved principal's sad demise and extended all of our collective sympathy to the bereaved family. School would be closed the following day so that we could, if we desired, evince the above-mentioned sympathy by our appearance at the funeral. Date and location were announced.

She then swung into a more familiar routine of club meetings, unsigned tardy slips, and illicit behavior in halls and rest rooms between classes, all of which made her tidy little world go round.

I went to the teachers' lounge for a shot of caffeine. As I entered, Evelyn caught me by the arm and pulled me back into the hallway. "I need your help," she whispered. "We're going to get Pitts. The filthy slime has gone too far, and I'm going to expose his nastiness once and for all. Now that Weiss is no longer around to protect him, Pitts will get exactly what he deserves."

It was mystifying, but certainly more interesting than Miss Dort's announcements or the watery coffee in the lounge. Evelyn was flushed with anger; her dark eyes sparkled with an expectancy that bordered on mayhem. Once I had nodded my acquiescence to whatever she had in mind, she hurried into her classroom and returned with her student teacher. The quivering girl was told to go into the ladies room in the lounge and make a production of checking her lipstick and hair in the mirror.

"Is Pitts in the ladies room?" I asked.

"Worse. I'll show you where the beast is—and what he's doing."

She led the way around the corner into the dark area of the hallway where I'd had the conversation with the Latin pedant.

We entered the custodian's door and tiptoed through a labyrinth of paper towels, murky mops and buckets, odoriferous boxes of disinfectants, and the other paraphernalia necessary to combat youthful slovenliness.

Beyond the storage room was Pitts's private domain, a dismal room with a chair, a coffee table, and a sagging cot covered with a tattered blanket. Yellowed pinup girls gaped over their exposed anatomies, pretending astonishment at having been snapped in such undignified poses. The calendars below were from former decades, but I supposed Pitts hadn't noticed.

In one corner was Pitts himself. He failed to notice our entrance, in that he had one eye and all of his attention glued to a hole in the wall. Evelyn glanced back at me to confirm my perspicacity as a witness, then crossed the room and tapped his shoulder.

He spun around, his lips shining moistly in the dim light. "Why, Miz West! What're you all doing in here?"

"The more important question is: What are you doing, Mr. Pitts?"

"Nothing. Gitting ready to mop the hall like I always do on Monday morning. Then I got to repair a broken window in Mr. Weiss's office and see about the thermostat in the girls' gym. Don't want those girls to get cold in them skimpy gym suits, do we?"

"Imagine all that work. Wouldn't it be more entertaining to peek at the women teachers in the ladies room?"

"Now, Miz West," he began in an awful whine, "I don't know why you'd say something like that. I wouldn't never——"

Evelyn brushed him aside with one finger and put her eye to the hole. "What a delightful view, Pitts. I'd always presumed you received your jollies smoking dope with the sophomore boys, but now I see you've branched out into visual amusements as well. I am going upstairs to report this to Miss Dort, the superintendent of schools, the head of custodial maintenance, the school board, and anyone else who will listen."

"Now, Miz West——"

"You will be dismissed, Pitts, and it will be a day of celebration for the entire school. A holiday, with dancing in the halls, followed by a touching ceremony in which you will be literally booted through the back door, never to be seen here again."

"I didn't make this hole. I jest found it and was trying to see where it went is all I was doing, Miz West. That's the honest-to-gawd truth—I swear it." He ducked his head and shuffled his feet in a cloud of dust. I waited to see if he actually tugged his forelock in classic obsequiousness, although it would have had to be unglued first. He settled for the expression of a basset hound put outside on a cold night.

Evelyn gave him a cold look as she joined me in the doorway. We left the room and made our way back to the hall, Pitts's sputters and whines drifting after us like a breeze from a chicken house.

"Brava," I murmured. It had been impressive.

She was shaking with anger, but her expression held a hint of satisfaction. "I meant every word of it. That filthy man is finished at this school and at every other school in the system. He can go clean sewers, which is what he deserves. On the other hand, I deserve a medal, a bouquet of long-stemmed roses presented by a lispy, angelic child, and a year's sabbatical to Paris to brush up on my vocabulary."

"When did you notice the hole?"

"This morning, but I have no idea how long it's been there. It almost makes me ill. Not only could he watch us adjust panty hose and hike our skirts, he could probably hear every word said in the lounge when the door was ajar. Lord, I feel the need of a shower, or at least a rubdown with disinfectant."

I was in the midst of agreeing with her when the bell rang and students exploded into the halls. I retreated to the journalism room to meet my first-period class. Said group was silent and soberly watchful as I entered the room and sat down behind the desk. It took me a moment to recall that they were freshmen— and we all knew whom the freshmen had chosen as their candidate for Weiss's murderer.

After some deliberation, I decided to let things stand as they were. It did keep the class under control, in that they seemed to feel it necessary to watch me for signs of imminent attack upon their persons. I tossed over the roster book and leaned back to think about the murder, since I, armed with the wisdom of age and the inside track, knew the freshman class was mistaken.

I had reached no significant conclusions when the bell rang and the class galloped away. The second-period class came, milled around quietly, and left at the bell, as did I. The lounge was empty, which suited me well, and I was dozing on the mauve-and-green when the sound of water in the kitchenette roused me.

A Fury entered the main room, a porcelain cup and saucer in hand, and offered me a timid smile. Tessa Zuckerman had not been seen since her collapse during the distasteful events of the potluck, and Mrs. Platchett was difficult to confuse with anything except, perhaps, a bulldozer. Therefore, I deduced that it had to be Mae Bagby. And Caron swears my mental capacity is changing in inverse proportion to my age.

"How is Miss Zuckerman?" I asked. "Has she recovered?"

"She's still in the hospital, and the doctor wants to keep her a few more days. She hasn't been well for several years, you know, because of female problems, and her strength isn't what it ought to be." The Fury perched on the edge of a chair, her back rigidly erect, her knees glued together, and her ankles crossed at a proper angle. She looked dreadfully uncomfortable, especially to someone sprawled on a sofa. "We are taking up a collection to send her flowers," she continued in a thin waver, "although you certainly wouldn't be expected to donate anything since you hardly know her."

"But I would be delighted," I said. It was one of the perils of aligning oneself with any group, from secretarial pools to construction workers' unions. Someone's always being born, married, or buried—all of which require a financial contribution from coworkers. "Is there also a collection to send flowers for Mr. Weiss's funeral?"

Mae Bagby turned pale, and the teacup began to rattle as though we were in the early stages of an earthquake. "Bernice is taking care of that, I'm sure. Bernice is very efficient about that sort of thing. You might inquire in the office later in the day, or wait until there is a mimeographed note. There is one almost every day during sixth period. The collection for Tessa is a more personal gesture from those of us who frequent this lounge, our little group."

One of whom was apt to have poisoned Weiss. Before I could mention it, Miss Bagby stood up and drifted into the kitchenette to dispose of her cup and saucer. She then visited the ladies room (I hoped Pitts had retired from peeping), gave me another timid smile and a cozy wave, and left the lounge in a flurry of faint creaks from her crepe-soled shoes.

Once she was gone, I found myself wondering if she had really been there, or if I had hallucinated the presence of a shade, a ghost of teachers past. All schools were likely to have a few in the darkest corridors, moaning at the transitory fads and disintegrating moral standards. Rattling lockers at midnight. Reading faded files of students long since departed, in both senses of the word.

I was getting carried away with my Dickensian reverie when I was saved by the bell. Evelyn and Sherwood came in the lounge, followed by Mrs. Platchett and Mae Bagby, who was still insubstantial enough to warrant a second look. Once everyone opened Tupperware, took sandwiches from plastic envelopes, fetched drinks, and found seats around the table, I asked Evelyn if she had reported the custodian to Miss Dort.

"Yes, I did, but I don't know what's going to happen to him, and I really don't understand." She told the others what we had discovered during homeroom, which produced a considerable amount of outrage from all except Sherwood, who looked smugly amused.

"What did Bernice say?" Mrs. Platchett demanded.

Evelyn sighed. "She was horrified, naturally. Then she said things were too chaotic to deal with the problem immediately, and once we settled down she would inform the proper authorities. I presumed *she* was the proper authority. I put tape over the hole, but I won't feel comfortable in the ladies room until Pitts is gone—permanently."

"Nor shall I," said Mrs. Platchett. "I am surprised that Bernice did not react with more forcefulness. Surprised and disappointed, I must add. I could never determine why Mr. Weiss tolerated Pitts's slovenly work and disgusting presence, not to mention the possibility that he was corrupting some of our students. One must surmise Mr. Weiss had his reasons. Bernice should know better."

"What is Pitts rumored to be doing with students?" I asked.

Sherwood waved his pipe at me. "It's all speculation, of course, and the man has never been caught *in flagrante delicto,* but it is whispered in the hallways that Pitts operates a major retail operation from his lair. Not only is it said that he peddles ordinary cigarettes and alcohol, but also that he has such things available as funny cigarettes and contraceptives. Names of abortionists for students caught with their panties down."

"And this is tolerated?" I said, appalled by both the information and Sherwood's blasé tone of voice. "The custodian is allowed to sell illegal things to the students and send them to back-alley abortionists—and no one objects?" I stared at the teachers busy with their lunches. "Why hasn't someone reported him to the police? Don't you care?"

"I said those exact things," Evelyn said. "We've all repeated the gossip over and over again to Weiss. He always promised to investigate. When we tried to follow up, he would say that there was no proof, and that he couldn't fire Pitts or go to the police on the basis of idle gossip, especially from a bunch of students with big mouths and bigger imaginations."

Mrs. Platchett nodded. "He went so far as to imply that we also had oversized imaginations. It was monstrously insulting to those of us who have dedicated ourselves to the education of youth, and I was forced to say so on more than one occasion. I even showed Mr. Weiss proof that Pitts went through the refrigerator during class time, touching our food with his germ-ridden hands and helping himself to whatever caught his fancy."

I hadn't exactly warmed up to Mrs. Platchett in the past few days, but I felt a good deal more kindly toward her now. "What did Mr. Weiss do?"

"Nothing, Mrs. Malloy. He did nothing."

Miss Hart and her coach came in to the lounge, both aglow with young love and/or hunger. She greeted all of us with a warm smile, but Jerry continued into the kitchen and began to feed coins into the soda machine.

"I say, Finley," Sherwood called, "we're all dying to know what Weiss had on you. Be a good chap and share the secret with us. We swear we won't say a word to Mrs. Malloy's policeman."

"Can it, Timmons," growled a voice from the kitchenette.

Sherwood rolled his eyes in feigned surprise. "*Cave canem,* particularly those with sharp teeth and rabid temperaments."

"Leave him alone, please," Paula said earnestly. "It wasn't anything important, and Jerry doesn't want to talk about it. Mr. Weiss wasn't going to do anything; he was just—being difficult about a minor issue." She turned on the warm smile once again to convince us of her sincerity and unflagging faith in her coach. "Would anyone like some of my salad? I made the dressing myself."

Jerry stomped out of the kitchenette with a bottle of soda and a brown bag. "Don't you have a secret of your own, Timmons? Weiss's comment about the library sounded as if he knew something about you—something you might not want to get spread around the school. Did you kill him to keep him quiet?"

"Or did you get him first?" Sherwood sneared.

"Really!" Mrs. Platchett gasped.

"Jerry!" Paula Hart whispered.

"Sherwood!" Evelyn West muttered.

"Oh, my goodness," Mae Bagby sighed.

I, in contrast, did not make a sound. But I was scribbling notes on my mental clipboard faster than Miss Dort in her prime could have ever done. And praying I had every word down.

The remainder of the lunch period passed in silence. Each teacher tidied up and departed with noticeable haste. There were no companionable farewells. I made it through the rest of my classes without incident, although I cold-heartedly denied Bambi's request that she and the staff be allowed to return to the printer's to remind him the newspaper would not be forthcoming. The blue slips were too much to think about. My darling daughter kept her nose in her algebra book, pretending she was a motherless child. Thud and Cheryl Anne did not appear during their appointed hour; I marked them absent without a qualm.

During the last few minutes of the last class, a mimeographed page was delivered. It proved to be a missive from Miss Dort, containing information about the flower collection, a thinly-veiled threat not to miss the funeral, another about blue slips, and a final paragraph about the homecoming game and dance. Which was, I realized as a chill gripped me, slated for the immediate Friday. Miss Dort would not spend the week in search of a better-qualified substitute, since she would be occupied with the duties of assuming command, even if in a temporary capacity.

It was inescapable: I was going to chaperone the dance unless I solved the murder and resolved the journalism accounts in the next four days, in which case Miss Parchester could resume her duties and I could cower at my bookstore. It did not strike me as probable, considering the quantity of suspects, the wealth of opportunities, and the dearth of motives. I made a note to purchase shin guards and earplugs, not to mention a tranquilizer or two, and a stun gun, should the crowd go wild.

I was still brooding that evening when Peter came by. For reasons of his own, he was back to being Mr. Charm Himself. He stirred up a little warmth (he can, if he wishes, be quite adept), then politely asked if he might be presumptuous enough to request beer and sympathy.

I opened the beer, reserving judgment about the sympathy until I figured out what he was up to. "Any luck in the investigation?"

"I spent most of the day in Weiss's office, but it was a waste of time. Jorgeson says he feels more acned with each hour we spend in that damn place, and I'm beginning to feel the same way. I don't know how anyone can stand it."

"The teachers are a sincere lot. They've got to be dedicated to put up with the bureaucracy and low pay. There was an odd conversation today during lunch, by the way." I told him about Sherwood's crack and Jerry Finley's retort. "Both of them seem to have secrets that Weiss knew and was using to needle them. Did you find anything about either of them in the personnel files?"

"Nothing that I intend to repeat to a civilian who is not sticking her lovely nose into things that are off-limits."

He made a amatory lunge for the civilian, but she wasn't having any of it. "Then you did find something," I said excitedly. "What was it—criminal records? Falsified credentials? Accusations from parents about incompetency? Was it something serious enough that one of the two would actually poison Weiss to stop him from exposing it?"

"There was nothing significant in anyone's file. Okay?" He tried a feint and a second lunge, but I slithered from under his arm and gave him a cool look.

"If you think I believe that, Peter, then you underestimate me. You will regret it, especially when I solve this case and prove Miss Parchester innocent of everything, from embezzlement to sloppy bookkeeping to murder. Your aversion to sharing information may slow me down, but it won't stop me."

"Would being locked up as a material witness stop you?"

"Not on your life." Which is precisely what it would cost him, along with beer, sympathy (should it be proffered at some future date), successful lunges, and incredibly witty conversation with a red-haired bookseller. He wouldn't dare.

"S"E"V"E"N"

The school was closed the next day for Weiss's funeral. Caron and I attended, as did a large crowd of faculty members and a fair number of students. The minister intoned the phrases, Cheryl Anne and her mother sniffled into sodden tissues, and Jorgeson (Peter's minion) watched impassively for hysterical, guilt-inspired confessions. We were at last dismissed, our ritual imperatives satisfied. Afterward, Caron announced she intended to spend the afternoon at Inez's house in the pursuit of algebraic mastery. She departed in a self-righteous glow that failed to impress me.

I decided to see if Miss Parchester had recovered from my last visit. I doubted I would be allowed to speak to her, but it seemed as good a plan as any on a lovely autumn day. I changed out of basic drab and drove out to Happy Meadows, determined to storm the bastion, or at least request an audience.

To my surprise, the guard let me in after a perfunctory search of car and purse. Person was not mentioned. I parked under a yellow oak and went inside, wondering if the inmates had taken over the hospital and declared a holiday from Anabuse and cucumber sandwiches. The sight of Matron shattered my fantasy.

"Well," she said with a frigid smile, "have we decided to bring our patient back so that we can try to recoup what ground we've lost?"

"We have no idea what you're talking about. I've come to speak to Miss Parchester." A sinking feeling crept over me as I studied Matron's less-than-cordial expression. "You haven't lost her, have you?"

"We do not lose patients."

"Do we misplace them?"

"It is possible that Miss Parchester has seen fit to leave Happy Meadows without being dismissed by her attending physician. It is most improper for her to do so, and she must return immediately so that the paperwork can be completed and her bill finalized. The insurance work alone takes hours to process."

"When did Miss Parchester leave, and how on earth did she get past the goon at the gate?"

Matron cracked a little around the edges. "We don't know exactly. We are certain she did not exit through the gate, since it is always locked at ten o'clock. Her room was empty this morning. She had arranged some pillows under her blanket to give the impression that she was sleeping peacefully, and I fear the night staff did not actually enter her room after midnight rounds. They have been reprimanded, and there will be notations made on their permanent records."

"But Miss Parchester managed to creep out of here at some point during the night and scale a ten-foot fence?" I said incredulously. "It's ten miles to town, and it was damn chilly last night. Did she have a coat? Have the grounds been searched? Did you call the police?"

My voice may have peaked on the final question, for the white-coated doctor came out of his office to investigate the uproar. When he saw me, he stopped and pointed his finger at me. "You are the woman who claimed to be an attorney! You put my patient in hysterics for several hours after your visit, and undermined hours of intensive therapy. I'm sure your visit was responsible for her subsequent actions. What have you done with her?"

"I haven't done anything with her, buddy. You people are supposed to take care of her, not allow her to stumble away on a cold, dark night. You'd better pray she didn't fall in a ditch somewhere and freeze to death! Then you'll have more attorneys around here than orderlies with butterfly nets and nurses straight out of *One Flew Over the Cuckoo's Nest*." I took a deep breath and ordered myself to stop frothing at the mouth. "Now, what have you done to find her and get her back?"

"Doctor has done everything possible," the Matron began ominously. I presumed she'd seen the aforementioned movie—and rooted for the head nurse. "He has followed policy."

Doctor's eyes avoided mine, and his fingers intertwined until they resembled a tangle of albino worms. "Thank you, Matron. I have indeed done everything to locate the patient. We have sent attendants out to search the estate, but we have nearly two hundred acres of meadows and woods. We fear the presence of the police may frighten the patient if she is hiding in the underbrush, so we have not yet called them."

I was torn between demanding they call the police and agreeing that they shouldn't, self-preservation being one of my primary instincts. My conscience finally won. "You'd better call the police immediately; your patient may be wandering down some back road in a daze. Ask for Lieutenant Rosen. He's been wanting to speak to Miss Parchester. . . ."

Doctor, Matron, and I exchanged uneasy looks. Doctor took a folded slip of paper from his pocket and handed it to me. "This was found on her pillow this morning during six o'clock rounds. Perhaps you can make some sense of it."

The spidery scrawl was hard to read, but I made out references to Bernstein, Woodward, and freedom of the press. I sank down on a ladderback chair and propped my face in my hands. Miss Emily Parchester, I bleakly realized, had taken up investigative reporting. Her reputation and her recipe for brandied peach compote were at stake. She was determined to expose a murderer and thus clear her name, along with the Judge's. But where was she now—and what was she doing?

I jerked myself up. "Before you call the police, I need to make one call. In private."

Doctor escorted me to his office. I dialed Inez's number, praying the girls would still be there. Inez's mother, a bewildered woman who has no inkling of her daughter's antics, assured me that they were in Inez's room, and soon I had Caron on the line.

I told her what Miss Parchester had done, then asked her to go to the escapee's neighborhood and watch for her to amble down the sidewalk in pink bedroom slippers. After warning her about the likely presence of a policeman on a similar assignment, I told her to call me at home if anything happened.

Caron was enchanted with the idea of playing detective. She suggested a disguise; I ruled it out and suggested she pose as an innocent teenager. She announced that she would be utterly terrified to go alone. I agreed that Inez was the perfect codetective for the stakeout. I refused to think up a code word, then hung up in the middle of a melodramatic sigh.

When I came out of the office, Doctor was hovering nearby, his fingers in a hopeless snarl. "I suppose we'd better call the police," he said, "even though the publicity will be most detrimental to our program. The newspapers will delight in hearing we've let a patient slip out of our care, particulary an elderly one in inadequate clothing, but I suppose it can be avoided no longer. I shall have the Matron place a call to this Lieutenant Rosen."

I shrugged a farewell and went out to my car. On the way home, I drove down Miss Parchester's street and then past the high school. Several little old ladies were out cruising, but none of them were slipper-shod. I pulled up in front of the house, planning to wait by the telephone in case Caron or Miss Parchester called, but I could not force myself out of the car. I knew who the first caller would be, if he didn't come by in person to harangue and harass me. Withholding evidence. Conspiracy to aid and abet an alleged felon. Bad attitude. Lack of trust. Tuts and sighs.

"Phooey," I muttered as I pulled away from the curb and drove back to the high school. Maybe Miss Parchester would attempt to find sanctuary with one of her old chums, who was apt to be a comrade. If I could get in the building, I could get addresses from the files and make unexpected visits. It was preferable to positioning myself for the inevitable, tedious, sanctimonious lecture. Some of which, I admitted to myself, just might be justified, if one ignored the humane element. I wouldn't, but others might.

There was a single car in the faculty lot. The main doors were locked. I took out my car keys and tapped on the glass until I saw a figure glide down the hall toward me. The sound had been adequate to rouse the dead; I hoped I hadn't. The figure proved to be Bernice Dort, clipboardless and less than delighted to let me into the building.

"Whatever are you doing here, Mrs. Malloy?" she asked once I had been admitted a few feet inside.

A bit of a poser. After a moment of thought, I said, "I came by to pick up the pages for the layout. I seem to have left them in the journalism room yesterday afternoon. So silly of me, but I'm a novice at this yearbook business."

She gave me a suspicious frown, but finally nodded and adjusted her glasses on her nose. "I presume it won't take long for you to fetch the pages and let yourself out this door. Make sure it locks behind you. I shall be in the third-floor computer room should you require further assistance. In the middle of tragedy, Mr. Eugenia continues to muddle his midterm data cards."

I waited until she had spun around and marched upstairs, her heels clicking like castenets in a Spanish café. "Thank you, Mr. Eugenia," I murmured as I hurried down the hall to the office.

The room directly behind the main office was crowded with black metal filing cabinets. As I expected, one was marked "Faculty/Staff." I was tempted to settle down with a stack of folders, but I was afraid Miss Dort might click into view at any moment.

I found the two marked "Platchett" and "Bagby," copied the home addresses on a scrap of paper, and eased the drawer closed with a tiny squeak.

My mission complete, I decided I'd better find a handful of layout pages (if I could identify them) in case I encountered Miss Dort on exit. The stairwell was gloomy, but not nearly as gloomy as the basement corridor. Some light filtered in through the opaque windows of the classroom doors, and an "exit" sign at the far end cast a red ribbon of light on the concrete floor. A boiler clanked somewhere in the bowels of the building.

I reminded myself that outside the sun was shining, birds were chirping, good citizens were going about their business. My fingers may have trembled as I turned the knob, but I did not intend to meet any psychotic killers or even any adolescent bogeymen. I switched on the light, snatched up a pile of old newspapers and a few pieces of graph paper, switched off the light, and started for the stairs and daylight.

When I heard music.

Country music, those wails of lost love and broken dreams in the best Nashville tradition. It came from the far end of the hall, in the proximity of the teachers lounge. Screams, groans, or howls would have sent me leaping up the stairs like a damned gazelle. Nasal self-indulgence did not.

Frowning, I crept down the hall and stopped in front of the lounge door. The music was indeed coming from the lounge, and below the door there was a stripe of light. The music faded, and a disc jockey reeled off an unfamiliar title and a tribute to some dead singer. A female vocalist began to complain about her womanizing lover.

It was not the stuff of which nightmares are born. As I opened the door, I considered the possibility that Miss Parchester had chosen the lounge as her port in the storm, and I prepared a bit of dialogue to convince her to return to the meadows.

There was a congealed, half-eaten pizza on the table. An overturned glass lay beside it. A puddle of glittery stickiness looked, and smelled, like whiskey. Another smell hit me, a very unpleasant one that was familiar. An image of Weiss vomiting during the lethal potluck flashed across my mind, unbidden and decidedly unwelcome.

"Miss Parchester?" I croaked. "Are you here?"

The female vocalist began to wail with increased pathos for her plight. I snapped off the transistor radio. "Miss Parchester? It's Claire Malloy, and I've come to help you."

Silence. The smell threatened to send me out to the corridor, but I gritted my teeth and moved toward the rest room doors. The men's room was empty. The ladies room was not. Pitts, the reptilian, slimy, disgusting, filthy, incompetent custodian, would never again be berated for failing to wipe down a chalkboard or mop a floor.

I went upstairs to the office and dialed the number of the police station. I asked for Peter, naturally. I told him what I'd found in the teachers lounge, then suggested he trot right over before I had hysterics. I hung up in the middle of the eruption and went to find Miss Dort in the great unknown called the third floor.

We were at the main door when the police armada screeched up, blue lights, sirens, ambulance, and all. Peter shot me a dirty look as they hurried past us, but he did not dally to congratulate me on my discovery and quick-witted action. Jorgeson settled for an appraising stare; he did not seem especially surprised to see me. One would almost think Peter had mentioned me on the way over.

Miss Dort and I followed them down to the lounge. She was white but composed, although her lips were tighter than a bunny's rear end. "This is dreadful," she said as we entered the room. "Pitts was despicable, but he did not deserve this any more than Herbert did. Someone is on a rampage and must be stopped. The students will be panicked by—" She broke off as Peter came out of the ladies room. "Mrs. Malloy seems to think Pitts was also poisoned with cyanide, Lieutenant Rosen. Is this true?"

"Mrs. Malloy has many thoughts; however, she seldom shares them with me," he answered. The smile aimed in my direction lacked warmth, as did his eyes. His voice might have halted a buffalo stampede.

"I called you immediately," I pointed out.

"Did you consider calling me from the Happy Meadows Home?"

There was that.

"Of course I did," I lied smoothly. "The doctor there said he would call you; it would have been redundant."

"It would not have been so four days ago. It would have been enlightening."

There was that, too.

"If you had asked me if Miss Parchester was at Happy Meadows, I would have told you." I decided to change the subject before it detonated. "Was it cyanide?"

The look he gave me promised future discussion, but Miss Dort's presence deterred him at the moment. "Probably so, but we'll send samples to the state lab. It looks as though it was introduced through food or drink."

We all stared at the table. "I would guess it was in the whiskey," I said. "I can't imagine poisoning pizza . . . unless someone sprinkled powder in the mozzarella, or slipped it under the pepperoni. But Pitts must have brought the pizza with him, which would make it all the more difficult. It would be much easier to dump poison in the whiskey bottle and leave it in the lounge. Pitts probably thought it was Christmas in November."

Peter was unimpressed by my well-constructed theory. "What an expert you've become in the modus operandi of murder, Ms. Malloy. How unfortunate the department can't afford to hire you, but thus far you've provided your services at every opportunity and at no charge, haven't you?"

Miss Dort interrupted his petty tirade. "This must be stopped, Lieutenant Rosen. The school will be in an uproar until this killer is apprehended, and the students will be unmanageable. As temporary principal, I have a duty to the school board and the community to operate this school efficiently and with a minimum of disruptions to the educational process. You can't believe how the press has hounded me—the calls—the interference from administrative paperwork to the ceiling—I don't know what I shall do."

Peter took her by the arm and escorted her to the lounge door. "I'll post an officer at the main door tomorrow to keep out the press, and I'm sure the administration people won't blame you for this. For now, show me the personnel file on the victim. I'll need his home address and next of kin, along with whatever there is about his past work record and personal data." He turned to glare at me. "Ms. Malloy, I will require a statement from you, but not at this time. Wait at your residence."

"Certainly." There was no reason to argue about the directive, not when I intended to ignore it. "I shall await your arrival with bated breath, Lieutenant Rosen. Do you need to write down my address?"

He sighed, shook his head, and left with Miss Dort. I guessed I had ten minutes or so before they returned, so I perched on the mauve-and-green and tried to look inconspicuous. In that my face was still greenish, it was moderately successful. The photographers snapped numerous rolls of film, and the fingerprint men dusted surfaces. The medical examiner came out of the ladies room, his face as green as my own despite his years of experience. Jorgeson directed traffic.

"Jorgeson," I said sweetly, "have you received the analysis from the lab concerning the cyanide that killed Herbert Weiss?"

"I guess it won't hurt to tell you it came from an organic source rather than a manufactured process. The Gutzeit test confirmed the presence of the compound in the peach compote, but we've asked for further tests to pinpoint the precise source." He scratched his chin. "Did you know peach pits contain cyanide, as do apple seeds, cherry pits, apricot pits, and a whole bunch of fruit like that? Gawd, I used to eat apple cores all the time. It seemed tidier. Gawd!"

"I suggest you throw them away in the future," I said without sympathy. Time was of the essence, in that Peter was apt to be displeased if he returned to find me grilling his minion. "Are we assuming the cyanide came from peach pits?"

"I don't think the lieutenant wants you to assume anything, Mrs. Malloy. He'd probably demote me if he found out I even talked to you. You'd better run along and wait for him at your house."

"I shall run along. Don't worry about demotion, Jorgeson; there's no reason why the lieutenant should ever know about our little chat, is there?" I gave him a beady look, then gathered up the newspapers and graph paper and went upstairs, wondering if Miss Parchester's recipe included such toxic ingredients as peach pits. Surely it would have been noticed over the years.

I took a few turns in the corridor to avoid the office. Once in my car, I checked the addresses and drove to Mrs. Platchett's house, a respectable little box in a respectable little neighborhood. She came to the door in a bathrobe, her head covered with bristly pink rollers. "Mrs. Malloy," she said through the screen, "how interesting of you to drop by unannounced. Is there something I can do for you?"

I considered a variety of lies, then settled for the truth about Pitts's untimely demise and Miss Parchester's escape from Happy Meadows. She was appalled, although it was difficult to decide which bit of information caused the greater grief. It proved to be the latter.

"Emily is wandering around Farberville with some wild notion that she will investigate Mr. Weiss's death?" Mrs. Platchett said, shaking her head. "Great harm is likely to happen to her. She is too trusting for her own good, and easily taken advantage of by anyone who claims an interest in the Constitution. You must locate her at once, Mrs. Malloy."

"I thought she might have come to you." I peered over her shoulder at the interior of the house. "Are you sure she's not hiding in a back room?"

"She is not here." Unlike some of us who shall remain nameless, Mrs. Platchett was not amused by the idea that she would aid and abet an alleged felon. "If you wait on the veranda, I will call Mae and see if she has heard from Emily, but it is almost inconceivable that she would make contact with either of us, and Tessa is still at the hospital. Emily knows we could not hide her from the authorities. It is against the law, and possibly unconstitutional."

I nodded. "Please don't bother to call Miss Bagby. Her apartment is on my way home, and I can stop by to speak to her in person." I hesitated for a minute. "Ah, do you happen to have any peaches, Mrs. Platchett? I know it sounds strange, but it may help Miss Parchester."

Unconvinced and visibly in doubt of my sanity, she disappeared into the house and returned with a lumpy brown bag. She handed it to me and watched through the screen door as I climbed in my car and drove away.

Mae Bagby invited me in for a cup of tea, although she did so in a listless fashion, murmuring that the funeral had drained her. I told her about Pitts. She closed her eyes, then took a swallow of tea and said, "This is truly dreadful, Mrs. Malloy. First poor Mr. Weiss, and now Pitts. Whatever are we to do?"

"The police will be unobtrusive tomorrow and finished with the crime scene by the next day. I suppose the students will appear to seek knowledge and the teachers to offer it to them."

"I don't know if I can bear to return to the school," she sighed. "It's not only the events of the last few days that motivate me to consider early retirement from my profession. The school has changed so much in the last forty years, and always for the worse. The students are so unconcerned about academics and morals, and they blithely break the law by consuming alcohol and drugs. Some of them actually engage in sexual activity to the point of promiscuity. It is all I can do to interest them in biology, in the discovery of the glories of nature. Perhaps I shall inquire about retirement."

I made a sympathetic noise, then asked if she had chanced upon the errant Miss Emily Parchester. Miss Bagby was as perturbed as Mrs. Platchett, but as firm in her avowal that she could not, under any circumstances, however justified, friendship or not, hide a fugitive. I gave her my telephone number in case the fugitive appeared, patted her shoulder, and drove home to conduct an experiment worthy of a Nobel Prize.

I was sitting on the sidewalk with the peach and a hammer when Peter pulled up to the curb. He almost smiled at what must have been a peculiar picture, then remembered his role as Nasty Cop. Slamming the car door hard enough to spring a sprocket, he stomped up the walk and glowered down at me. "I called earlier, but you were not here. I thought I told you to go home and wait for me."

I took a bite of peach. Yummy. "You did. What if I've been sitting out here since I arrived home?"

"I drove by several times."

"It takes me awhile to scurry home with my tail between my legs." I wondered where Mrs. Platchett bought her produce. Peach juice dribbled down my chin. I wiped it on my sleeve, finished the last bite of peach, and picked up the hammer. "I'll account for my whereabouts in a moment, but first I want to see how hard it is to get out the pit."

"And why would you want to ascertain that information?" he snapped, unmoved by my quest for knowledge.

"Peach pits contain cyanide; everyone knows that. Because the peach compote contained an organic cyanide compound, it does seem probable that the pits are implicated—if they're not impossible to extract."

"Not everyone knows the chemical structure of peach pits. When did you chance upon it? High school chemistry—or more recently?"

Lacking an acceptable answer, I ignored the remark and smashed the seed with a mighty blow. It bounced into a pile of dried leaves. "Damn, this is harder than it looks," I said as I crawled across the walk and started to dig through the leaves.

Peter leaned over and picked up the peach pit. "Let me try," he said in a grudging voice—since he hadn't thought up the brilliant experiment.

I handed him the hammer and sat back to watch him smash the seed. His expression was enigmatic, to say the least, but his single blow was forceful enough to shatter the outside covering and expose an almond-shaped pit. He studied it for a second, then handed it to me. "It isn't difficult. Anyone could do it."

"Not little old ladies with tremulous hands and poor eyesight," I said. "It takes the male touch to pulverize an innocent pit. We of the opposite persuasion lack the temperament. I really can't see delicate Miss Parchester on her hands and knees on the sidewalk, smashing peach seeds to collect the pits."

"Ah, Miss Parchester. Couldn't you have told me where she was—before she disappeared? You knew damn well that I wanted to question her, Claire. The fact that you knowingly failed to tell me her whereabouts borders on a felony."

As Mexico borders on France. "I felt responsible for her," I admitted in a wonderfully contrite voice. "I thought I could clear things up before you dragged her to the station to book her."

"But instead you lost her. Now she's playing Miss Woodward-Bernstein, and liable to dig herself into more trouble. If we'd had her tucked away in a cell, she couldn't have been a suspect in the custodian's murder. But of course she's trotting around town, no doubt with a purse full of compote and peach pits, and might have visited the high school during the funeral. I've issued a warrant. Good work, Ms. Malloy."

"Thank you, Lieutenant Rosen." I snatched up the hammer, put the pit in my pocket, and started for the house. "I'll give you a call when I determine who really killed Weiss and Pitts. In the meantime I have to wait for an important call."

"I have to take your statement. Now."

I faltered in midstomp. "No more sarcasm. I confuse it with the warm glow that comes from impacted wisdom teeth."

We went upstairs. He took my statement, then apologized and made amends. I accepted the apology, allowed amends, and generally forgave him for his boorish behavior. But I then shooed him away, worried that Caron might call while he was there. An apology was one thing, Miss Parchester another. And I *was* going to clear her name.

"E"I"G"H"T"

Caron's vigilance was not rewarded. She complained about it straight through dinner, then retreated to her room to sulk in solitude when I failed to offer adequate sympathy. I spent the night envisioning Miss Parchester supine in a pond or ditch, her slippers atwitch in her death throes. It did nothing to contribute to sleep, and I was not in a jolly mood the next morning as I arrived at what threatened to become my permanent classroom. I longed for the Book Depot, the jackhammer, my crowded office, the antiquated cash register with the sticky drawer, and the rows and rows of lovely books. It didn't do a damn bit of good.

Farberville High School had not closed its doors to commemorate the death of a custodian. During the morning announcements, Miss Dort assigned a few terse words to the tragic loss of an employee, warned the students not to speak with reporters, and went right on to the homecoming festivities—the very mention of which gave me goose bumps. I went right on to the lounge.

There were traces of fingerprint powder on the table and a lingering aroma that someone had attempted to overpower with pine-scented air freshener. I felt as if I'd been teleported to Maine. I contemplated a search for the other lounge, which to my knowledge was not yet a breeding ground for corpses, then reminded myself that I would learn nothing there. I waded through the pine cones and poured myself a cup of coffee.

Paula Hart came into the lounge. After a warm smile of greeting, she started for the ladies room, then stopped and shook her head ruefully. "I can't do it," she said with a small, deprecatory laugh. "I intended to be quite sensible about it, since the other faculty lounge is so far. But I can't make myself go in there—not after what happened to poor Pitts."

"You're the only person who's apt to be distressed by Pitts's death," I said. "Everyone else will celebrate—in a decorous manner, of course."

"He was a sad little man. He did so want to be a part of the staff, but he simply did not fit in with us. No education, a certain lack of—of physical fastidiousness, an inclination to grovel that encouraged certain people to ridicule him without mercy. All those rumors about him, based on student gossip, which can be fanciful. Heaven knows they come up with some wild ideas at times. The others were ready to lynch him, but I tried to give him the benefit of the doubt. I suppose I felt sorry for him."

It occurred to me that she and her coach had entered the lounge after the discussion of Pitts's peepery. I asked her if she knew about the spy hole in the ladies room.

"Evelyn told me. I wish I knew how long the hole had been there. I'd like to think he wasn't watching me adjust my panty hose every morning, but we'll never find out." She made a face. "It is awful, isn't it? Being spied on through a nasty hole in the wall. . . ."

"He was also privy to conversations when the door was open," I told her, making the same face but with a more mature set of wrinkles. "I guess he overheard quite a lot of personal conversations."

She fluttered a hand to her mouth. "Oh, I don't think he could hear anything, do you? Even with the door open, it's a thick wall and there's always noise in the halls."

"Let's test the hypothesis," I said, enamored of the idea of yet another Nobel-level experiment, this time in acoustics. "I'll go in his closet and put my ear to the wall. You take the tape off the hole, then go into the lounge and talk. We'll find out if he could have heard anything."

"What shall I say?"

"Anything. Your name and address. The alphabet."

She looked doubtful, but she stayed in the middle of the room. I went around the corner and through the storage room to the private sanctum. There were signs the police had examined the room, and I wondered if they'd found the alleged stash of illegal substances. I wryly noted a collection of empty whiskey bottles. Pitts would have done better to stick with his own brand.

I located the hole and put my ear to it, feeling rather sleazy even though I was conducting research for a good cause. I heard Paula chanting the alphabet as if she were inches away. Acoustical miracles, I supposed. Paula broke off in the middle of "L-M-N-O."

"Hi, Jerry," she said brightly.

"Why are you in the middle of the room reciting the alphabet?" he asked, not unreasonably.

I could almost hear the flutter of her hands. Our Miss Hart was not, to her credit, an accomplished liar, but it seemed she couldn't bring herself to expose me. Or maybe the truth was too silly for her true love to be saddled with.

"For a typing test," she gasped. "Third period. I'm going to time them on the alphabet."

"And you're not sure you remember it?" He chuckled at her, then cut off her flutters with what I presumed was a kiss. "Listen, my darling, I've got to find that blasted transcript before the police do. No, don't interrupt, please. If the police stumble onto it, they'll think I had a motive to murder Weiss. Honey, let me finish. I doubt it's in the regular file; Weiss wanted to dangle it over my head like a damned sword before he made it public. Maybe it's hidden in his—*what?*"

There was a long silence, punctuated by earnest whispers and a low growl. The door of the ladies room slammed shut, thus leaving the location of the mysterious transcript unspecified and my left eardrum aquiver in tympanic shock. I felt fairly sure Jerry wasn't going to offer further details, no matter how nicely I asked.

I was still listening to chimes in my head when I heard a noise through the hole. I waited a few minutes, then leaned against the wall once more, prepared to sacrifice scrupulosity and dignity in exchange for information. A toilet flushed, water ran in the sink, and the door was opened—and left ajar. Someone more considerate than the coach was in the lounge. Footsteps, the clink of the coffee pot against a mug, more footsteps. I decided the odds on a killer admitting all, particularly to a room devoid of an audience, were nil to none, and I was on the verge of abandoning my post when someone laughed.

"How's your student teacher faring in the face of all this mayhem?" Sherwood said. "Is she more *non compos mentis* than usual?"

"I suspect she'll flee back to the college to find another major." Evelyn sounded as if such flight held appeal. "The rest of us will end up with *delirium tremens,* complete with hallucinations and crazy ideas that this place isn't really a temporary stop on the way to the morgue. Policemen underfoot, newsmen in the parking lot, and Bernice Dort in command. Oh, Sherwood, I can't believe anyone would murder Herbert Weiss, or even pitiful Pitts. Maybe I am losing my mind."

"Surely you are not devastated by the loss of our *factotum,* our worthless dogsbody? We'll get a replacement, and we'll be better off for it, as will the building and the ignoble savages. By the way, I have arrived at a startling insight, Evelyn—one that warrants serious cogitation. It involves Pitts's vile habit of eavesdropping through that little hole. It must have been the precise size to accommodate his mind—which contradicted the tenet that *natura abhorret vacuum.*"

I did not take it personally.

"What do you mean, Sherwood?" said Evelyn. "And get to the

point without any incomprehensible asides, please. The first-period bell is going to ring any minute."

"It seems to me that certain information conveyed in confidence wormed its way upstairs to the domain of our resident Zeus. It has now been demonstrated that the walls have ears—perhaps they also have mouths."

"I understand your Latin better. What, Sherwood?"

"Among his other virtues, Pitts must have been a snitch. You heard Weiss's crack about the library, Evelyn, and only you and I knew about that matter. How else could he have learned of that absurd accusation, unless Pitts overheard our conversation and tattled to his boss?"

I willed him to explain. He didn't.

"That may be," Evelyn said, "but it's irrelevant now. Weiss and Pitts are both dead, so it doesn't matter what either of them heard. It's very convenient for you, isn't it?"

"*Mutatis mutandis,* a change for the better. May I presume my secret is safe with you, Evelyn?" There was a pause during which I prayed for a brief reiteration of said secret. There wasn't. "Ah, good, I knew I could trust you. We'd better retreat before the halls swell with the undeodorized."

A door closed. I rubbed my ear as I tried to make sense of the tidbits I'd heard. I did understand why Pitts eavesdropped; the conversations were entertaining and provocative, if not lucid. All I had to do was determine the meaning and what bearing, if any, these secrets had on two cases of murder. A transcript and an accusation about a library. Was either worthy of murder?

The bell jangled. I realized it was time for the first period and made my way through the outer room. I opened the door—and crashed into Sherwood Timmons.

"My goodness," he said, tugging at his goatee, "what have we here? Have I caught you *in flagrante delicto,* Claire?"

"You have caught me in the hall—and on my way to meet my first-period class. Now, if you'll excuse me, Sherwood, I must—"

"I fear I must insist you explain your presence in Mr. Pitts's closet. Were you seeking clues, or listening to your elders through a convenient hole in the wall?"

"Don't be absurd. I simply wanted to take a look around, to see if the police overlooked anything of importance."

"Overlooked—or overheard?" He moved forward until I could smell the wintergreen of his breath. "I had thought better of you, held you in the highest esteem, idolized your famed deductive prowess. Now I wonder if my Athena is but a mortal, as flawed as the rest of us."

"I am indeed flawed, but my vices do not include tardiness. It's first period, Sherwood, and I must meet my class."

"We shall meet again," he said, bowing slightly.

He stepped back and I hurried away, as pink as a small child caught in the vicinity of a forbidden cookie jar. A misdemeanor, but still embarrassing. I survived the first two classes by debating whether to tell Peter what I'd heard—or overheard, anyway. It was moot. On the one hand, he would be gratified that I cooperated, for once. On the other, he would not be gratified that I was still investigating. In mystery novels, the amateur sleuths are not hindered as they sniff around for clues and analyze casual remarks for Freudian slips. The police share all the evidence and are unflaggingly grateful for what assistance they receive.

I concluded that Peter needed to read more fiction, after which I might consider cooperating with him.

The second-period class wandered away, and I went to the lounge to ponder the puzzle. I was pondering away when Evelyn came in.

"What a nightmare," she said once we were settled cozily over coffee. "Especially for you, since you found the body. Why were you in the building yesterday afternoon, Claire? Did you really come back for the yearbook layouts?"

The speed with which gossip spread through the school was astounding, but I was beginning to get used to it. I told her about riffling the files for Mrs. Platchett's and Mae Bagby's addresses, and the reason for doing so. And the subsequent failure to find Miss Parchester at either residence. I did not tell her that I had also stained my jeans with peach juice, and allowed Peter to prove his manhood with a hammer.

"Poor Emily," she sighed. "She is so unpredictable, and I hope she doesn't do anything rash in the name of freedom of the press. It's her guiding force in life; she'll defend it to the death, murmuring about the Judge all the while."

"To the death?"

"No, that was hyperbole. But she is devoted to the cause, which resulted in a lot of rumbling about the *Falcon Crier*. There were some stories that were outrageous, filled with misinformation, adolescent ravings, and controversial stands on taboo subjects. I know Weiss bawled Emily out on several occasions, but she refused to censor anything her apprentice reporters wrote."

"Do you think this Miss Demeanor nonsense has anything to do with the murders? Most of it was drivel, but the business about the Xanadu Motel was different." I chewed on my lip, trying to recall a snippet of conversation that seemed as if it might have meant something. It remained steadfastly out of reach, like a mosquito bite in the middle of one's back.

Evelyn was staring at the wall. "It doesn't have anything to do with what's happened in the last week, Claire. I can't explain, but it really is irrelevant."

"Why can't you explain?"

"It was just a tacky little attempt on someone's part to stir up trouble," she said. "Once the newspaper was halted, so was the smear campaign. There's no point in worrying about it now."

I chewed off the rest of my lipstick, then said, "It was blackmail, wasn't it? You've got to tell me what it meant, Evelyn. It could be important, and I must know who was blackmailing whom—and why." When she shook her head and looked away, I took the obvious shot. "Do you and Sherwood visit the Xanadu on a regular basis?"

"I'm single, and so is he. We both live alone, so we would hardly pay for a sleazy motel room for an afternoon romp, would we? And even if we did, it wouldn't be much of a crime. A scandal, perhaps, but not a very big one in this day."

"Then who?" I demanded, forcing myself not to grab her by the shoulders and shake it out of her. I liked her, although her recalcitrance was straining the friendship. Caron evokes the same emotion in me.

"I can't tell you. You'll have to trust me when I say that it has no connection to Weiss's murder. It would make no sense whatsoever, and letting the gossip spread is unconscionable."

I let it go for the moment, although I wasn't prepared to accept her word. "Then let me ask you something else. What did you think about Weiss's comment in the teachers' meeting about Jerry's transcript? Is it possible that he falsified it, that he didn't really graduate and doesn't have a degree?"

"I don't see how," Evelyn said. "He has to have state certification to be employed as a coach and teacher, and the district office keeps the necessary forms on file. The state board of teacher certification grinds exceedingly slowly, but it does grind and cannot be avoided. I just thought Weiss was needling our golden boy, most likely out of petty jealousy."

"He did needle him well. I'd like to get a peek at the personnel files, though. There has to be something peculiar about Jerry's transcripts; he stormed out of the meeting and said some harsh things about Weiss afterward."

"Did he?" She studied me as if I had admitted poisoning the city water supply, then went into the ladies room and locked the door.

The bell rang (it was beginning to regulate my life) and the other faculty members appeared shortly for what proved to be a very restrained lunch period. Mrs. Platchett and Miss Bagby both gave me inquiring looks. I shrugged and shook my head to the unspoken questions. Ignoring me, Jerry sulked his way through a sandwich and left, despite Paula's unhappy sighs. Sherwood winked, but I managed to avoid an unseemly reaction; he did possess a key and I a healthy curiosity about the personnel files. Not to mention the journalism books, which I'd almost forgotten.

I retreated to the journalism room for fourth period. When Caron sauntered in, I tossed the roster to Bambi and beckoned for Caron to join me in the darkroom.

"Can you go to Miss Parchester's neighborhood after school?" I asked her. "I doubt she'll show up, but I don't want her to fall into the sticky arms of the law if she does."

"I wasted an entire afternoon there yesterday, Mother. It was Utterly Boring, and I see no point in putting myself through that ordeal again. Besides, Inez and I have to work on the Homecoming float."

"What Homecoming float? Is there to be a parade?"

"I was not referring to coke and ice cream," she sniffed. "The parade is Friday afternoon at three o'clock, and each class has to enter a float. The freshman entry is 'Broast the Bantams.' It's dumb, but no one could come up with anything remotely clever. We're working on it, stuffing crepe paper in chicken wire and that sort of thing, in Rhonda Maguire's garage."

"A float is not as important as Miss Parchester," I began in a sternly maternal voice. I realized that Caron was about to insist that it certainly was, if not a good deal more so. "All right, go work on the float. But if Miss Parchester is arrested for murder, you will not be writing the Miss Demeanor column next week. Or next year, or eons down the road when you're a senior. Keep that in mind while you're ankle-deep in crepe paper."

I left her to mull over her thwarted career and sat down at the desk to mull over my thwarted scheme. And my next move. Bambi McQueen approached, a sly look on her face. "If you'll write me a blue slip, I can take the absentee list to the office now, Mrs. Malloy. It's supposed to be turned in right after the beginning of class. Miss Dort doesn't like for it to be late."

"By all means," I said. I opened the desk drawer and took out a pad of blue slips. I noticed a key among the pencil stubs, a rusty thing with a tag marked "mailbox—office." "Does this open the Miss Demeanor box?" I asked with a flicker of interest.

Bambi said she thought it did, and I handed it to her with instructions to bring the contents of the box back with her. She waited until she had her trusty blue slip in pocket, then bounced away with a smug expression. Her expression was glum when she returned, however, and I was prepared for the announcement that the box was empty.

Once school was over, I walked slowly to the parking lot, not sure where to go, or what to do when I got there. Miss Parchester was not likely to appear at her apartment, and I had no theories about where else to search for her. A policeman of certain familiarity hailed me before I could reach a decision and beat a retreat.

"I have a message for Miss Parchester," said Peter. He leaned against my car, his arms folded and his smile deceptively bland. "Good news, actually."

"I'll be happy to pass it along when I see her," I said, miffed that he would think I was hiding her. Did he think I had her stashed in the trunk—or tied up in the attic?

"I brought in an accountant do a quick audit of the journalism books."

"Oh, did you? That was terribly clever of you."

"Thank you. The fact that you were involved in the matter gave it more significance than one would normally give it."

"Thank you. I didn't realize my presence was quite so ominous."

"Your presence is always ominous. Ominous, omnipresent, and according to some rumors, omnipotent."

"As much as I've enjoyed this repartée, I have more important things scheduled for the remainder of the afternoon," I said through clenched teeth. "What did the accountant find in the journalism books? If you're not going to tell, do it now."

"The accountant said that the books were basically in order. He said there had been crude attempts to make the account look short, but that the money was all there. He had a few other comments about Miss Parchester's system, which he found peculiar yet amazingly sound. I suspect she'll be relieved to find out that the embezzlement charges are going to be dismissed."

Leaving the minor matter of murder. "Who fiddled the accounts to make her look guilty?"

Peter shrugged. "I suppose I could hunt up a handwriting expert, but all he'd have to go on are a few smudgy numbers penciled in over the originals. Do you honestly think this has anything to do with the murders? A few dollars missing from a club account, easily located once the books are examined?"

"No, not really. It's damned odd, that's all . . . and it did result in Weiss's death. If Miss Parchester hadn't been accused and exiled, she wouldn't have left the compote in the lounge, thus providing someone with the vehicle to poison Weiss. I keep thinking it had to be planned; one doesn't stroll about a high school with a pocketful of peach pits."

Jorgeson appeared around the corner of the building and yelled at Peter.

"I'm needed," he said, charmingly reluctant to desert me. "Will you swear you don't have Miss Parchester tucked away somewhere?"

I dutifully swore (since I didn't), and went so far as to invite him to come by later in the evening. We parted amiably. I drove to the hospital to visit Tessa Zuckerman, the only Fury I hadn't questioned. I did not expect to find Miss Parchester hunched under a hospital bed, but I was running out of potential ports.

Miss Zuckerman resembled a limp, faded rag doll in the bed. Her arms were crowded with needles and tubes; her face was almost the color of the pillowcase that engulfed it. She appeared to be asleep, but as I started to tiptoe out of her room, her eyelids fluttered.

"Mrs. Malloy?"

"Hello, Miss Zuckerman. I came by to see how you were. Don't let me disturb you if you need to rest."

"No, it was so very kind of you to come, and I'm flattered by your concern. You must tell me the truth, Mrs. Malloy. Mae and Alexandria have taken it upon themselves to protect me from any outside news. Their decision is admirable but frustrating. They will tell me nothing about the dreadful—occurrence in the lounge. How is Mr. Weiss?"

I hedged for a moment, then told her. She closed her eyes for a long time, and I had decided she was asleep when she at last stirred. "Thank you for telling me," she said. "I wondered as much; he looked so ill and the bluish cast to his skin made me think of cyanosis. Have the police arrested anyone for the crime?"

"No, but they would like very much to speak to Emily Parchester about the brandied peach compote. They have not been able to find her, however. Has she been to visit you in the last few days?"

She turned her face away from me, and her voice took on a guarded tone. "I get so confused, Mrs. Malloy, that I cannot be sure whether my visitors are real or imagined. Let me think. . . . No, Emily has not been here that I can recall. I doubt she intends to come."

It was as convincing as Paula Hart's explanation of why she was standing in the lounge reciting the alphabet. Jerry might have believed his beloved, but I knew a lie when I heard one. And I'd just been offered a whopper.

"Please tell her I have good news—should she come by," I said. "I'll see you when you come back to school." Her eyes were closed again, but this time her breathing was deep enough to indicate that she had fallen asleep. I stopped at the nurse's station. "How is Miss Zuckerman doing?" I asked a shiny-faced young thing.

"As well as can be expected, but renal failure is very, very serious. Are you a member of the family?"

"In a way. Does her doctor have any idea how long she'll be in the hospital?"

The young thing gave me a long, solemn look. "The patient is not expected to recover," she whispered. "The endometrial cancer is no longer in remission. No other forms of treatment, including the less conventional ones, have had any significant effect, and she has refused further chemotherapy."

I forgave Tessa Zuckerman for her lie. I made a mental note to send flowers while they could be enjoyed, then thanked the nurse and walked out to my car. A woman nodded as she walked past me, a box of candy in her hand. A worried young man with a child hurried by, followed by an elderly couple and several teenagers. I gaped at their backs. Visitors. Emily Parchester had visited her dying friend, and would do so again.

The next set of visiting hours were from seven to nine P.M. I needed a couple of bodies for the stakeout, since I would have to entertain Peter. I drove to Rhonda Maguire's garage and steeled myself for both the incipient outrage and the sight of "Broast the Bantams." Neither would present a pretty picture. I was right on both counts.

After a hefty dose of cajolement coupled with money for hamburgers and milkshakes, Caron and Inez abandoned their class-mates and left for the hospital. If Miss Parchester appeared, she would be tailed by two excited detectives with crepe paper in their hair.

When Peter came by, he was too tired to discuss the case. We drank wine and watched television like old married folks, and he was actually nodding when the telephone rang.

I grabbed it before the second ring. "Yes?" I hissed.

"Mrs. Malloy? This is Inez. Caron told me to call you and report what happened."

Peter's head was still lowered. I turned my back to him and hunched my shoulders around the receiver. "What happened, Inez? Why did Caron tell you to call? Why can't she come to the telephone herself?"

"She is in the emergency room. Even if she could call, I don't think she's in the mood to talk about it."

"What is she doing in the emergency room? What happened?"

"It's a long story, Mrs. Malloy, but Miss Parchester finally showed up at Miss Zuckerman's room. We were waiting in an empty room across the hall, ready to tail her to her hideout." She gulped several times. "Then, just as Miss Parchester started to go in Miss Zuckerman's room, a nurse spotted us and yelled at us to come out and explain what we thought we were doing."

"There must be more, Inez. Please get to the reason that my daughter is now in the emergency room and unable to speak to me."

"Miss Parchester jumped about ten feet when she saw us. Caron grabbed her to try to tell her that we wanted to help, but I think it must have scared her. Anyway, she sort of bopped Caron on the head with her umbrella and ran away down the hall."

"And Caron has a concussion from being assaulted by an old lady with an umbrella?"

"Not exactly," Inez said, sighing faintly. "Caron and I both started after Miss Parchester, but the nurse got in the way and we all ended up on the floor. Caron sprained her ankle. The hospital security people put her in a wheelchair and brought her down here to get it taped. I don't think they're going to let us go, Mrs. Malloy. My mother is going to kill me."

"No, she's not," I said. I could envision the fiasco from start to finish, from the lurkers in the dark room to the current extension of my daughter's lower lip.

"I have to go," Inez said in a very small voice. "They won't let me talk anymore. Will you bring bail, Mrs. Malloy? Caron and I have less than a dollar, and I think we're in worse trouble than that."

I assured her that I would be there within ten minutes and replaced the receiver. Peter was still asleep. There was no way to explain where I was going and why. There was also no reason to try, so I opted to let sleeping dogs lie. Better than I.

I left a note on his wineglass and tiptoed out the door.

"N"I"N"E"

I managed to extricate Caron and Inez from the clutches of hospital security, but it took an insurance card, a parental consent form to X-ray and subsequently wrap a twisted-but-not-sprained ankle, and an endless stream of avowals that neither girl would set foot in the hospital again unless they were preanesthetized in the parking lot. During all this fun, Caron limped out of a cubicle and shot me an icy look.

"This has been So Entertaining," she said. "It was all your idea, Mother. I told them that much, but they wouldn't listen to me. Anyway, I don't see how you can trespass in a public building. They Do Say this is a public building, don't they? That means the public can come in, doesn't it? I am public, aren't I?"

Nostrils aquiver, she beckoned for Inez to support her. The two hobbled out the door, leaving me to fill out insurance forms under the reproachful scrutiny of a nurse, who seemed to think I was some sort of modern day Fagin. Which I suppose I was.

There was a good deal of sniffing and puffing in the car, but no further rhetorical rampages or comments on culpability. Inez muttered a thanks for the ride and scurried into her house like a leaf caught in the wind. The inarticulate outrage continued all the way to Caron's bedroom door, where I was informed she could manage quite well without me. No thanks for the ride, either.

Peter was gone, saving me from the necessity of producing explanations (lame/mendacious) for the errand and for the noises that still drifted through the bedroom door. I made a cup of tea and retired to my bedroom to think about Miss Parchester. My theory that she would visit Miss Zuckerman had been right, but she had slipped away without divulging the location of her hideout. And she wouldn't return to the hospital. The debacle in the hallway would fuel her paranoia. I seemed to have perfected the ability to both find her and lose her. I considered what Peter would do if he ever found out about the scene in the hospital, when the fugitive had fled into the great unknown—again. In all probability, he would not be amused.

I went on to Pitts's murder, and wasted a good fifteen minutes wondering why he'd been poisoned. Sherwood suspected the custodian had carried tales to the principal, who then used the knowledge to apply pressure to various members of the faculty. Could Pitts have indulged in a spot of blackmail on his own? I glanced at the *Falcon Crier,* trying to imagine Pitts as the author of the nasty letters. Not Pitts, I concluded, although it would have been charmingly tidy; he hadn't been capable of penning insinuations and innuendos of such delicacy. Pitts had been, I thought glumly, more of a crayonist.

But his murder had to be linked to Herbert Weiss's death, which lacked any motive I could determine. Weiss hadn't been popular with the teachers I'd met, and probably wasn't any more popular with the other faculty members, but someone had taken an extreme view of things. Who? Pitts hadn't won any popularity contests, either. The rumors might be true, or they might well be the ravings of postpubescent imaginations. The same minds that evolved the concept of "Broast the Bantams" could surely assign nefarious motives to what might be innocent situations. I caught myself in a shudder.

The Homecoming festivities could no longer be ignored. After a gulp of tea to give me courage, I tapped on Caron's door. "May I come in, dear? I need to ask you something."

"Does it involve leaping off a cliff to help you with your investigation? Organ donation? Defenestration?"

Alert to the very real possibility of missiles being flung with lethal intent, I eased open the door. "Your ankle must be hurting. Can I bring you another pillow and some aspirins, or loosen the bandage? How about a nice cup of tea and some cookies?"

The patient was sprawled on her bed, the offending foot elevated on a pillow. Her glower had all the subtlety of a roman candle. "No thank you, Mother—you've done Quite Enough. I had to tell Rhonda I can't work on the float tomorrow afternoon, since I can barely walk. She demanded to know what happened. I had no idea what to say without thoroughly humiliating myself, so I made up some stupid story. I could tell she didn't believe me, and she'll tell everyone at school what a total klutz I am."

Better than the truth, which was likely to get back to certain cops alurk in the building. "Let's talk about the Homecoming schedule," I suggested, perching on the corner of her bed nearest the door. One never knows. "The parade is Friday afternoon?"

"Right after school at three-thirty, up Thurber Street and around the square. I was going to walk beside the float and do our class yell, but I doubt anyone will offer to push me in a wheelchair and I couldn't possibly keep up on crutches. The band would march right over me."

"You can see so much better from the sidewalk. Are you going to the game and dance? I need some advice about what to expect, and some support while I chaperone."

"Inez and I have to sell programs at the game to earn pep points. Maybe I'll sell more doing my Tiny Tim Cratchett imitation." She sucked in her cheeks and held out a cupped hand. "Please, sir, a penny for the crippled children's fund."

I almost laughed, but the sparks in her eyes kept me sober. "It will probably work, especially if you wear burlap. What about the dance? Are you and Inez going together—or do you have dates?"

The cupped hand went over her face, muffling the next words.

"No, I don't have a date, Mother. Some geek from my homeroom asked me, but the thought was nauseating. I told him I wasn't allowed to date until I was thirty. He's geeky enough to believe it. Inez and I haven't decided whether to go or not, but after Rhonda finishes telling everyone about klutzy Caron Malloy, I may not show my face in public again—ever."

"If you handle this carefully, you can win a lot of sympathy. You'll have all the boys waiting on you, bringing you punch and that sort of thing. It'll be fun."

"The geek will sit beside me all night, and I won't be able to get away from him," she sniffled. "I'll end up with pimples and herpes." She was already dialing for sympathy as I left her room.

The time had come for drastic measures if I was to avoid the Homecoming dance, save Miss Parchester's reputation, defend freedom of the press, discover the author of the Miss Demeanor blackmail letters, solve two murders—and keep Peter Rosen from locking me away for the rest of my life. I had forty-eight hours, tops. Or forty-eight years, if one used the actuarial tables.

I therefore yelled at Caron to get off the telephone, took several deep breaths, and called Sherwood Timmons.

After a round of diplomatic manuevers, I asked him if he was willing to let me in the high school that night.

"Ah, so you are still on the case of the fiddled books," he said, sounding delighted. "*Occasio facit furem*; the occasion makes the thief. Are we to wear rubber-soled shoes and use penlights to wend our way through the ledgers? Black turtlenecks and smudges on our faces? *Incognito et incognita?*"

"If you wish," I said meekly. Personally, I had on a wool jacket and my face was immaculate, but I decided to permit him his fantasies. The case of the fiddled books was no longer my primary motivation to search the office, since Peter had told me the money was still in the account. However, it seemed prudent to allow Sherwood to remain both incognizant and incognito, if he wished. I agreed to meet him in the darkest corner of the faculty parking lot. I then told Caron I had an errand and left her to continue her conversation with Inez about Rhonda—or Rhonda about the float—or the geek about hygienic distances—or something along those lines. She didn't even wave good-bye.

Sherwood loomed beside me as I climbed out of my car in the parking lot. "I must tell you how charmed I am by our little tryst, Claire. I do hope this will not be the only opportunity we have to get to know each other intimately. In fact, I've tucked a bottle of wine in my refrigerator in case we feel the urge for a spot of *vino veritas* once we complete our breaking-and-entering diversion."

I removed my elbow from his hand and gave him by best enigmatic smile. "We're merely entering, Sherwood, in that you possess a key. I realize it's unimaginative, but it's also less likely to get us arrested."

"Indeed. And we won't have to worry about the despicable Pitts appearing to fumigate, since someone has already exterminated him. *De mortuis nil nisis bonum*—but it is difficult not to interpret his demise as a gift from the gods."

"Then you believed all the rumors concerning drugs, alcohol, and back-alley abortionists? I was thinking about it earlier, but I wasn't around the school long enough to arrive at any valid conclusions about him."

"Only those on Olympus know for sure." He unlocked the door and held it open. "*Jacta alea est,* as Caesar was reputed to mutter; the die is cast."

The hall stretched like the interior of a monster, the lockers on either side glinting like rippled ribs. I hadn't cared for Sherwood's oblique reminder that we were alone, but I couldn't see him in the role of crazed poisoner. Praying my vision was accurate, I switched on my flashlight and led the way to the office and the file room beyond.

"Is this the most likely place to find ledgers?" Sherwood breathed on the back of my neck.

"Perhaps you should stay by the door in case someone's in the building," I said through the wintergreen haze. "Keep a lookout, listen for footsteps, that sort of thing."

I waited until he left, then found Jerry's folder and put it on top of the cabinet. After a quick glance through the doorway, I flipped it open and scanned it for dark, damning hints of an evil past or present. All I found was personal information of the innocuous sort, transcripts from Farber College and a midwestern university, and glowing recommendations from college coaches and professors. Jerry had maintained a high grade point average through graduate school, and had done nothing to disgrace himself that I could discover. Phi Beta Kappa and all that. No accusations of molestation or mismanagement of the team.

After a second glance through the doorway to confirm my sentry's position, I took out his file and looked at the contents. Nothing beyond the same sort of thing as in the coach's file. I closed the drawer and went into the main room. "I'm going to look through Weiss's desk," I whispered.

He nodded tersely. "I thought I saw movement at the end of the hall. Can't be sure. How much longer will you be?"

"Just a few minutes." I started for the inner sanctum, then stopped and went back to peer down the hall. "Did you really see someone down there? I don't especially want to be caught riffling Weiss's desk if there's a policeman in the building."

"Perhaps it's your policeman, dear sleuth. At least he wouldn't pull a gun on us and shoot us on the spot."

"Don't count on it," I murmured, deciding my lookout was too caught up in his assignment to be credible. I went into Weiss's office and sat down behind the desk. The drawers on either side were filled with forms, copies of memos, thick state regulation manuals, and other officious stuff. The middle drawer was crammed full of stubby pencils and confiscated goodies. A plywood paddle, worn shiny from use. Thumbtacks and ancient, lint-covered mints. A packet of letters held together with a rubber band—and addressed to that paragon of propriety, Miss Demeanor.

I jammed the packet in my pocket. And without a flicker of remorse, since they were already hot property, stolen from the journalism mailbox. By the principal, presumably. Who'd been murdered. Over a handful of letters?

My sentry coughed nervously. Ordering myself back to business, I dug through the drawer, but found nothing else of any significance. I went out and told Sherwood I wanted to take a quick look at Bernice Dort's desk.

He turned around, his face as garish as a Toulouse-Lautrec portrait in the spray of my flashlight. "One wonders if you're the least concerned about the journalism ledgers and poor Miss Parchester," he said softly. "*Prima facie,* one might think you're searching for something else, something to do with the faculty's private business. Now why would one arrive at that conclusion, my dear sleuth?"

I put my hand in my pocket. "I'm just checking things out, Sherwood. This is the first time I've been able to—to look around the office."

"For what?" He came toward me, his eyes inky shadows and his voice disturbingly calm. "Were you looking for something that might incriminate one of us? A letter, perchance, about me? Did you overhear a conversation in the lounge while you were innocently snooping in Pitts's sty?"

I edged around the counter, mentally cursing myself for the wonderful scheme that had landed me here—with him. I have an aversion to being menaced, particularly in a minty miasma. "I don't know anything about that, Sherwood. I went in Pitts's room out of curiosity, to see if there was any evidence that the rumors were true. I didn't eavesdrop at the vile little hole." Not much, anyway.

"*Suggestio falsi,* Ms. Malloy. I think you heard me discuss the distressful situation with Evelyn. That's why you looked so guilty when I caught you outside the room, and that's why you're suddenly so nervous, so worried that you shouldn't have come here with me, alone."

Bingo with a capital *B*. "Don't be absurd," I whispered, trying for an irritated edge to my voice. "I have no idea what you're talking about, and I don't want to know. If I thought you'd murdered Weiss or Pitts, I wouldn't have called you tonight."

"I would hardly murder Weiss over that idiotic accusation, even if I were perturbed that *vox audita perit litera scripta manet*— the voice perishes but the written word remains." He laughed, but it lacked a certain essence of mirth. "What's that you're clutching in your pocket?"

A diversion seemed timely, so I took out the packet and showed it to him. "I found this in Weiss's drawer, which explains why the journalism mailbox was empty. Why do you think he'd take the letters and stash them in his desk?"

"You'll have to figure that out on your own," he said, this time chuckling with some degree of sincerity. "Evelyn and I have wondered how long it would take the others—and particularly someone with your reputation—to deduce what's been happening."

"So you also know about the blackmail scheme?" I said. Enough retreating. I slammed down the packet and came around the counter, fists clenched, eyes narrowed. "Why won't Evelyn tell me the bare outline—if she's so damn sure it has nothing to do with the murders? For that matter, why won't you?"

"Because it's irrelevant, and Evelyn's determined not to encourage any gossip. She's gripped with some dreadful malaise called integrity; I tried to convince her otherwise, but she refused to tell me any of the juicy details, such as the identities of Aphrodite and her boyfriend. But she persisted, to my regret. Now, I do think we ought to depart before we get caught, don't you? I'd so hate to spend the night in the pokey."

I was about to persevere with the questions when a door

closed in the distance. Remembering my experiences a couple of days ago, with the music that led me to murder, I will admit I shivered—like a wet dog in a blizzard. "Did you hear that?"

My gallant sentry looked rather pale. "Someone in the building, obviously. A policeman?"

"Policemen don't prowl around in the dark. Earlier I wondered if Miss Parchester might have taken refuge in the building, maybe hiding in empty classrooms or closets until the building empties in the afternoon. I think we ought to take a look."

Ever so gallant, he gestured for me to precede him.

An hour later, we returned to the office. We'd been down every corridor, opened every door, peered into every nook (and there were a lot of them), and basically searched the entire building for the intruder. If Miss Parchester was determined to elude us, she was doing a fine job of it.

"Are you ready to leave?" Sherwood demanded, gallantry by now replaced with peevishness. "I have three sets of papers to grade, and we've wasted half the night. *Tempus fugit* when you're having fun."

I considered a lecture on the tedium of detection, but settled for a sigh. "Yes, let me get the Miss Demeanor letters and we'll go. I left them on the counter in the office."

The counter was bereft of packets. I checked my pockets and the floor. Sherwood swore he hadn't taken it, and even emptied his pockets to prove his innocence. After a further search and a great deal of grumbling, we left the building and went to our respective cars. *Vino veritas* was not mentioned.

I was still irritated when I arrived home, both irritated at myself for carelessness and at the unknown thief for tactlessness, among other things. I decided it would not be wise to ask Caron to stake out the high school the rest of the night. I confirmed that she was asleep, then picked up the last issue of the *Falcon Crier* to ferret out the identity of the nasty author if it took all night. *Tempus* might not *fugit*.

Dear Miss Demeanor,
  Why does everybody make such a big deal about dates, any-way? Two girls can have a better time, and not have to put up with a lot of yucky kissing and grappling from some Nauseating geek.

Dear Reader,
  Hang tight—someone will ask you out one of these days, and you'll discover the purpose of kissing and grappling, even with geeks.

After a deep breath and a moment of introspection as to my failure to provide adequate maternal guidance, I continued read-ing.

Dear Miss Demeanor,
  How contagious is mono?

Dear Reader,
  Contagious enough.

Dear Miss Demeanor,
  If you were supposed to provide moral leadership to a bunch of people, and you had a choice between being divorced for adul-tery and bending one teensy little rule, which would you choose?

Dear Reader,
  Miss Demeanor doesn't bend teensy little rules, because she has journalistic integrity. She doesn't stay awake at night worry-ing about being divorced for adultery, because (a) she's not mar-ried, and therefore (b) she can't commit adultery, even if she wants to. If driven to choose between such unpalatable options, she would probably climb in a closet and stay there. May I sug-gest the same for you?

I put down the newspaper and closed my eyes. It didn't take too long for the obvious to open my eyes, and eventually shove me to the telephone. I called Evelyn, apologized for the lateness of the hour, and asked if Herbert Weiss had been entertaining Bernice Dort in the Xanadu Motel every Thursday.

It took longer for her to respond, but at last she said, "I knew you'd figure it out, Claire. I had suspected as much since the first letter appeared in the Miss Demeanor column, but I saw no reason to speculate about it in the teachers lounge. They're both adults; they are entitled to behave however they desire—after school hours."

"But you're convinced of it now," I said. "You're not speculating any more. How can you be sure?"

"On the morning Weiss died, I was in the ladies room when they happened to come into the lounge. They discussed it rather loudly, I'm afraid. I would have preferred not to be there, but it was too late to show myself and pretend I didn't hear them. In any case, their affair couldn't have anything to do with his murder, so I chose not to mention it to the police or any of the faculty. Bernice wouldn't poison her lover, and there's no point in causing more grief to his family by exposing rather ordinary peccadillos."

"Well, someone else knew. If you weren't writing those blackmail letters—and I shall trust you weren't—then someone else was." I gnawed my lip until a fragment of conversation came back to me. "Cheryl Anne, Daddy's little princess, was the author. I happened to overhear her tell Thud that her scheme hadn't worked, that she would have to think of a new one."

"Weiss and Bernice didn't seem to know who wrote the letters, although I thought it was fairly obvious. I would guess that Cheryl Anne was hounding him at home to reinstate Thud, and using the column to keep him in a distraught frame of mind at school. The untimely cancellation of the newspaper put a stop to that. You don't think Cheryl Anne. . . ?"

"No," I said slowly, "I don't. I considered the possibility earlier, but the motive is feeble and the opportunity almost nil. After all, it's just a silly high school dance."

"You're one of the chaperones, aren't you?" Evelyn said. "Wait until you see how seriously they take these things before you dismiss it as a motive. Wallflowers have been known to transfer to other schools, and the intricacies of parking-lot misconduct dominate the conversations for weeks. But I think you're right about Cheryl Anne, Claire; surely she wouldn't poison her father over Thud's eligibility problems."

"Would Thud?"

"He'll end up in prison eventually, but it will be because of a barroom brawl, not a premeditated and well-planned crime. His mental limitations preclude that sort of thing. He'd be more apt to go after someone with a pool cue or monkeywrench, and in a mindless rage."

"That doesn't get us anywhere, then," I sighed. "It's tidier, but it doesn't get us any closer to discovering the identity of the poisoner. Cheryl Anne may have tried to blackmail her father, but she didn't poison the compote."

"Do the police still think Emily is the culprit? Have they been able to find her for interrogation, arrest, and execution?" Evelyn sounded as depressed as I felt.

I told her about the escape from Happy Meadows, the close encounter in the hospital, and the scene in the emergency room. Once she stopped laughing, she told me I ought to confess before Peter found out, interrogated, arrested, and executed a certain red-haired bookseller. She had a good point.

The next day my morning classes inched by without incident. The denizens of the lounge were almost mute during lunch, although Mrs. Platchett did report that Tessa Zuckerman was doing poorly. We all produced money for flowers and signed a gay little get-well card from "the gang at the office." She then gave me a questioning look, I shook my head, and we settled down to the soft whoosh of Tupperware.

Cheryl Anne did not appear during the Falconnaire period, presumably still in mourning over the demise of her paternal blackmail victim. Thud, presumably still ineligible, stayed hunched and unapproachable, although I wasn't sure with what I would have approached him. Or why.

Once I was free, I met Caron and Inez in the parking lot and drove them to Rhonda Maguire's garage, Caron having informed me she would At Least watch the work in progress. I went on to the police station, arranged a contrite expression, and asked to be admitted into the presence of Lieutenant Peter Rosen.

He closed his office door and put his hands on my shoulders to give me an unobstructed view of his eyes. The corners of his mouth twitched, but he gained control before he actually smiled. "To what do I owe the honor of your visit?"

It occurred to me that I really did like the man. It also occurred to me that I hadn't behaved well, and was apt to jeopardize the relationship if I continued on my blithe path. Getting a tad misty, I eased from under his hands and sat down on a battered chair. "I have come to confess all. You may then lock me up and swallow the key, but bear in mind that you will have to pick Caron up at five-thirty and fix dinner for her. She's incapacitated by a bad ankle, and I'm afraid her bark is as bad as anyone's bite."

He flashed his teeth at me as he sat down on the far side of his desk. "Before I order rabies shots, you'll have to tell me the extent of your crimes."

"The usual stuff," I said, squirming as if I were a teenaged truant facing Weiss's wrath and paddle. "Not mentioning little details to you, for instance. Prowling around the corridors in the dark to solve the murders and prove how clever I am. Evading the truth, although not as a rule."

"Are you going to elaborate?"

I elaborated for a solid thirty minutes. I told him how I'd been coerced into substituting, and why—which seemed to do odd things to the corners of his mouth. I recapped the conversations with Miss Parchester, the argument between Jerry and Paula after the teachers' meeting, the inexplicable comments I'd heard through Pitts's hole, the visits to the Furies, the hospital scene, the midnight prowl with Sherwood, and the enlightening discussion with Evelyn that led to the identity of the Miss Demeanor author. Then, making a face, I went so far as to admit how the letters had been stolen from under my nose. Not that they were still important, I mentioned in conclusion, unable to fathom the thoughts behind his expressionless face and somewhat uneasy because of it.

"You have been busy," he said. "Some of it I knew, and some I merely suspected, based on your track record. None of it surprises me, however, although for some naive reason hope springs—"

"Some of it you knew?"

He shrugged. "This morning hospital security reported an incident of minor importance. It did not require a brilliant flash of female intuition to guess the identity of two teenaged 007's in the room across the hall from Tessa Zuckerman, a witness in an investigation of particular interest to an unspecified party. The floor nurse related the details of the panicky visitor and the crazed attack that ended on the floor. One of the girls was rumored to be verbally precocious to the point the security men considered a tourniquet just below the chin. It was a good guess on your part, by the way."

"Thank you. What else did you already know before I came in here to grovel, apologize, and ultimately make a fool of myself?" I asked, resigned to the aforementioned trio.

"We asked the Xanadu manager for a description of his Thursday regulars, and he told us. No brilliance needed there, either. I discussed the affair with Miss Dort; I'm satisfied it was not a factor in Weiss's murder."

"Maybe she was jealous," I suggested. "Weiss was panting after Paula Hart, and we all know hell hath no fury. Miss Dort's efficient enough to crack a hundred peach pits in a precise row, grind the insides, put them in the compote, and shove a fork into her paramour's hand—all before the fourth period bell. There are likely to be notations on her clipboard."

"She said Weiss panted after women all the time, but that she was used to it and fairly confident after ten years that he lacked the balls to follow up on his lusting. She was scornful, not scorned."

I yielded for the moment, although I was not convinced. "You could have saved me a lot of trouble, you know. I had to learn all this the hard way."

"I'm not sure you ever learn anything, Claire." He shot me a discouraged look. "To continue, I also discussed the letters with Cheryl Anne, who was properly ashamed of her conduct and bravely offered to turn in her crown. Once she stopped sniveling at the idea, she pointed out that neither she nor Thud could enter the lounge without being noticed." He propped his feet on his desk, toppling a stack of folders, and crossed his arms. "That's pretty much what I've learned in the last few days. May I assume you've been equally open, despite your innate tendencies to the contrary?"

"You may assume so, Peter. I was trying to help Miss Parchester," I said, sighing. "I seemed to have muddled things more so than usual, and I'm sorry. If you're adamant, I will call Bernice Dort and tell her I won't be available to substitute tomorrow. No matter how deafening the jackhammer, I'll stay in the Book Depot and mind my own business. It needs minding, actually. I haven't been in for a week; the mice have probably invited all their friends in to nosh the paperbacks."

He rubbed his forehead, crossed his arms, rearranged the pile of folders, made noises under his breath, and generally allowed me time to suffer. I remained determinedly penitent. There were rumbles outside his office, cars coming and leaving, voices barking into telephones, lots of footsteps in the hall. All we needed were a few locker doors to be slammed, and we'd be in dear old Farberville High School between classes.

When I was about to exit with whatever dignity I could muster, he finally looked up and said, "You are convinced Emily Parchester is innocent. Despite your continual, maddening, eternally intrusive interference, I do value your opinion—if not your tactics. I suppose you might as well continue to substitute so that you can keep an eye on things in the lounge. You will, of course, report everything to me, without regard to your personal analysis of its value to the proper authorities."

"Of course," I murmured, somewhat disappointed I hadn't been ordered back to the bookstore for the duration. The thought had appealed. "May I be permitted to make amends to you?"

"Of course."

I gave him a bright smile. "Would you like to go dancing with me tomorrow night?" I suppose I might have mentioned the five hundred or so teenagers who would accompany us, but it must have slipped my mind.

"T"E"N

The events of the last week paled in the onslaught of the Homecoming madness. Most of the students wore some variation of red and gold in honor of the big day, and they chattered like starlings through the first two periods. The freshmen seemed to have either forgiven me for bumping off their principal or forgotten about it. No one paid any attention when I tried to quiet things down, so I settled for an aspirin and a long, solitary visit to the darkroom. Fourteen hours until the dance.

There were three bottles of aspirin beside the coffee pot in the lounge, standard equipment for such holidays. I gulped down another for luck, then slumped on the green-and-mauve, closed my eyes, and lulled myself with a pleasant reverie of books, bookracks, temperate bookbuyers, invoices, and quarterly tax estimates as yet uncomputed. The images evoked a quasi-religious rush of longing.

I kept my eyes closed as a few souls drifted in and out of the lounge, mission unknown. One was, I supposed, Evelyn's student teacher on her hourly breakdown; another was apt to be a Fury. I really didn't care. Now that Peter had asked for my help, I couldn't rally the energy to sniff out clues or grill suspects. *That* was too unsettling to think about, so I sank further into the plaid to doze.

"Burned out already?" Evelyn said in my ear. "Most of us survive a few years before we seek greener pastures elsewhere."

Yawning, I went into the lounge to get a cup of coffee. "I think it's psychosomatic," I called. "Anything to avoid chaperoning the dance tonight. The thought sends chills down my spine."

"You'll be in good company. Sherwood has the boys' rest room, Miss Bagby and I have the front door, and Jerry has the back door, to keep the smokers contained. Paula has the concession stand during the game, but I imagine she'll come with her beloved to ensure that he keeps his eyes on her and off the senior girls."

The coffee almost sloshed out of my cup. "Are you implying that Paula will attend this unspeakable function—even though she isn't required under penalty of death to do so?"

Evelyn laughed at my expression. "Paula's sweetness and light on the surface, but she has a stainless-steel interior. When she got fed up with Sherwood, she told him off with the acumen of a professional hit man, and he was so stricken he made nary a wisecrack in Latin for almost two weeks. It was truly amazing, not to mention refreshing. To everyone's regret, he finally recovered and is now much worse than before. I can count the Latinless sentences on one hand."

I stared at the formica table, trying to recall a bit of conversation that had occurred at the fatal potluck. "What did Weiss say to Sherwood about a manuscript that provoked a menacing Latin riposte?" I said, wrinkling my nose. "*Ars longa,* or something like that?"

"*Ars longa, vita brevis,*" Sherwood said from the doorway. "Art is long, life short. I didn't expect my delphic aside to be taken quite so literally by an unknown hand. Nor did I expect to continue to be your favorite suspect, Claire; I thought we'd resolved that last night, *in transitu.*"

"But have the sophomores abandoned you?" I said in a futile attempt to divert the direction in which we were aimed. It didn't work.

Evelyn raised an eyebrow at Sherwood. "Last night? I didn't

realize you two were getting all that cozy." She raised the other eyebrow at me. "You didn't mention anything when you called me to discuss the Miss Demeanor shenanigans."

Sherwood's eyebrows were up, so I raised mine, too, just to be companionable. "I asked Sherwood to unlock the building for me," I admitted. "I wanted to look at Jerry's personnel file to see if I could find whatever Weiss was holding over him. Sherwood was kind enough to comply, and we did discuss motives in passing."

"What did you find in Jerry's file?" Evelyn asked, thawing to early spring if not out-and-out summer.

I ignored Sherwood's glower. "I didn't find anything at all. It was all quite innocent—recommendations, teacher certification, good grades through graduate school, academic awards, that sort of thing. I was wrong when I hypothesized that he didn't have his degree. Degrees he has, and admirable ones."

Upon this seemingly innocuous revelation, Sherwood choked and sputtered through a mouthful of coffee and Evelyn turned an unbecoming shade of white. Both of them goggled at me as if I'd mentioned the coach's propensity for bestiality or the dismemberment of his first seven wives.

"What?" I said, unamused by their antics. "What's wrong with good transcripts and warm letters from old coaches?"

"Graduate school," croaked Evelyn.

"It's where you go after undergraduate school," I said. "I went to one myself, although I never got around to writing a dissertation. It's not a topic for 'The Twilight Zone' or 'That's Incredible.'"

"Jerry is a coach," Sherwood said, proving he too could croak. The pond was filling up; all we needed were lily pads.

"Jerry is indeed a coach, and probably a very good one," I said as tolerantly as I could. "He also has a doctorate in English literature, which is more than I can say after my three years of tuition, research papers, and white wine from a jug."

"A doctorate?" they croaked in unison. Lily pads couldn't be too far in the future, along with dragonflys and cattails.

"There's something you two aren't telling me. Why don't you calm down, sip some coffee, unstick your eyelids from your fore-heads—and tell me what you find so incredible?"

They looked at each other, shook their heads, looked at me, shook their heads, and looked at each other again. I was on the verge of an acerbic comment on the now-predictable pattern, followed by a repetition of my question in one-syllable words, when Evelyn found her voice.

"Jerry is a high school football coach. He's on the same salary scale as the rest of us, and it is determined by experience, contin-ued professional training—and educational level. No school would ever hire a coach with a master's degree, much less—" she gulped "—a doctorate, even if it were in physical education. He'd hardly warrant the top of the pay scale for two classes of general health, one drivers' ed, and study hall. They hardly hire any teachers with graduate degrees, since there are plenty with bachelor's floating around the market. So much cheaper that way."

Sherwood managed to find his voice, and it was laden with glee. "All Weiss had to do was call central admin and tell them about the degree, and our boy Jerry would find himself with his thumb out on the county line. *Empta dolore experientia docet;* painful experiences may teach, but not coaches with doctorates. Ooh, how delightful!"

"Sherwood," said Evelyn, "you do know you will not breathe one single word of this to anyone, don't you? If you so much as drop a hint in ancient Etruscan, I will call a press conference about your situation with that editor."

"The manuscript?" I prompted in a small voice, hoping they had forgotten my presence.

"*Et tu, Brute?* It was poppycock, and you know it," Sherwood growled at Evelyn. "Nothing was proven."

"It wasn't?" I said.

Sherwood grimaced so intently that his goatee trembled. "It sure as hell wasn't, Ms. Malloy. There was absolutely no basis for that slanderous allegation—everyone in my field uses the same reference texts and it's conceivable that a few phrases might sound somewhat similiar. Similiar—not plagiarized."

"An editor accused you of plagiarism, then returned your manuscript with a nasty letter?" I took a drink of coffee while I considered the implications. "Weiss found out, probably through Pitts's channel, and used it to make your life miserable and your career tenuous. You must have been furious."

Evelyn gave me a sad smile. "Sherwood told me about the letter the day after it arrived, and Weiss alluded to it for the first time that same afternoon. Sherwood's been frantic for weeks to learn how Weiss found out and what he intended to do, but it wasn't a motive for murder. The allegation was slanderous; it would have caused some degree of difficulty with other editors and certainly made it more of a battle to get published, but it wasn't life-and-death."

"No wonder you despised Pitts," I said to Sherwood.

His grimace eased. "I did. He was a despicable snitch, among his other qualities. He must have heard Jerry and Paula talking about the transcript and reported to Weiss, who simply sent for a copy. Holy Achilles, I wonder what Weiss had on the others. . . ."

"Something worthy of murder?" I said under my breath. The two must have heard me, for we all ended third period in a collective sigh.

At the end of the last period Caron informed me that I would have to drive her to the parade, since her ankle hurt and she wasn't about To Hobble Anywhere. As always, Inez was there to some degree. We parked behind the bank, made it to the square without too much hobbling, and found a flower box on which to sit.

Both sides of the street were beginning to crowd with students, parents, whiny children, and babies asleep in strollers. The sky was clear; the sunshine warm. I had about six hours until the dance.

Bernice Dort appeared behind us, sans clipboard. "How's your ankle?" she asked Caron. "I received a note that you were unable to participate in your physical education class, but one of the office monitors told me that you'd hurt yourself. I hope it's nothing too serious to prevent your participation in the freshman intramural volleyball tournament next week?"

Caron turned pink and said it ought to be better soon. Miss Dort nodded as if making a mental note to be transferred to a form, curled her lips at me, and started to march away.

I caught up with her at the curb. "This is my first parade," I said, despising myself for the ingratiating tone. "I understand the kids take the float competition very seriously."

"I am a judge, Mrs. Malloy, and I can assure you that *I* take the float competition very seriously. Class spirit brings the students together. It makes their formative years more meaningful, and encourages them to think fondly of their alma mater in years to come. I have not missed one of my class reunions in thirty years."

"Neither have I," I murmured as I crossed my fingers behind my back. Maybe I hadn't missed any of them; I'd never inquired. "You seem to be holding up well in the middle of all these tragic occurrences. The school continues to run well, and the students have already fallen back into their normal routines."

"Herbert Weiss was a great man as well as an inspirational leader of students and faculty. He will be sorely missed by all concerned." She leaned forward to peer around a pregnant woman. "It is three-thirty-seven now; the parade seems to be off schedule. Perhaps I ought to walk down the hill to find out what the problem is."

"Oh, they'll be along any minute," I said confidently. "I suppose you'll miss Herbert most on Thursdays."

She pulled off her glasses and watched them swing from the pink cord around her neck. After another glance around the pregnant woman, she pulled herself erect and looked me in the eyes. "I suppose I shall, Mrs. Malloy."

"You must have been panicked by the letters in the Dear Miss Demeanor column," I continued, "and willing to do almost anything to stop them. But framing Miss Parchester wasn't exactly the most humane route, was it? It caused all kinds of grief, and ultimately led to Mr. Weiss's murder."

"It was an unfortunate choice of actions."

"Your idea?"

"No, Herbert's. He was such an imaginative man. I do believe I hear the band in the distance; they're only eight and a half minutes late, which isn't too bad for this developmental stage. They do get caught up with themselves at times."

I heard the strains of an unfamiliar tune, but I wasn't about to be distracted by the promise of a parade. "So Herbert suggested you fiddle with the ledgers to make Miss Parchester look guilty, merely in order to halt publication of the *Falcon Crier*. The police have already determined that the money's been there all along."

"Neither of us condoned taking money from student accounts. That would be unthinkable, a violation of trust. Listen, they're playing a Sousa march."

"But it wasn't unthinkable to frame a little old lady who'd taught for forty years?" I said. Sousa be damned.

"Herbert had a truly creative mind," she said in a distracted voice as she tried to peer past the protruberent tummy. "It's surprising that he did not deduce the identity of the author of those letters. He could have disciplined his daughter at home, and saved both of us a great deal of worry, not to mention his time involved in devising and implementing the plan to stop the *Falcon Crier*. Luckily, my experience in bookkeeping proved to be a great value, although I was obliged to struggle with Emily's system before I could make revisions."

"What a shame to waste valuable time framing little old ladies."

"So we discovered," she murmured. "They'll probably begin the school fight song before they reach the square. It gives me tingles right down to my toes to hear the strains of 'Fight With All Thy Feathers, Falcons.' It's such a rousing tune that I just want to burst forth into song whenever I hear it." Her shoulders quivered with anticipation, and her lips lingered lovingly over the lyrics.

I wondered if she put equal enthusiasm and dedication into all her extracurricular activities. It was obvious that she and Herbert could have reached great levels of efficiency, if not ardor, in their lovemaking. Did she record climaxes on a monthly basis, with little checks and/or x's? I decided that she filled out all the "How-was-the-service?" cards and mailed them to corporate headquarters, even when postage was not guaranteed.

The crowd gasped at some unseen spectacle. Bernice stood on her tiptoes, straining to catch her first glimpse of the big event.

"Miss Dort," I said in a stern voice, "has it occurred to you that Emily Parchester is out there somewhere, frightened and alone, ashamed that someone might consider her guilty of a dastardly crime?" When I received a perfunctory nod, I upped my volume to compete with the growing noise of the crowd. "You did that to her, simply to cover up your affair. You've driven her into hiding, and I for one am terribly worried about her."

"If she knew she was innocent, then she shouldn't have poisoned poor Herbert."

"She didn't poison poor Herbert!"

"Who did?"

"Well, you might have," I said. "You might have slipped into the kitchenette and dumped powdered peach pits in the compote."

The pregnant woman turned to stare at us, then spun around and waddled away in an indignant huff. Bernice moved closer to the curb, but glanced back with a tight smile. "I had no reason to murder Herbert Weiss, Mrs. Malloy. I do not wander around educational institutions with powdered peach pits in my pocket, nor do I slip into kitchenettes to sabotage little jars of peach compote. I have personal standards."

"Prove it," I snapped.

"You prove it, Mrs. Malloy. I have floats to judge, and I do think I can see the tippy-top of the junior effort. Someone told me, in the strictest confidence, naturally, that its theme is 'Barbecue the Bantams.' Very clever, don't you agree?"

I glared at her back, which was all I was offered. When that paled, I returned to the flower box and sat down next to Caron. She and Inez made several unkind comments about the junior effort, and more about the Homecoming court creeping by in convertibles. The girls looked faintly blue in their low-cut gowns, but their smiles remained steadfast and their waves gracious. Cheryl Anne was in the last car, ever the modest reigning royalty of FHS despite the two kindergarten children on either side of her. The boy was wiping his nose on Cheryl Anne's dress; the girl openly bawling.

With a hint of satisfaction, Caron explained that they were crown bearers. It rather reeked of child abuse, but I let it go. The mayor went past in an antique car, followed by a junior-high band playing an arrangement never before heard by human ears. The sophomore float proved to be "Make Baked Beans of the Bantams," which Caron and Inez found, amidst giggles and snorts, Too Juvenile for words.

In the middle of this, I thought I saw pink bedroom slippers flash by in the crowd across the street. I poked Caron and muttered, "Look over there. Could that be Miss Parchester?"

"That is the drill team, Mother. Bambi McQueen's in the third row, and she can't even shake her pom-poms in the correct sequence. She's doing red-gold-red-gold, while everyone else does red-red-gold-gold. Her knees are too low, her hemline's crooked, and she has dumpy thighs. I don't know why they let her on the drill team."

"Over there by the post office door," I insisted, despite an urge to assess Bambi's thighs for dumpiness. "I can't see any faces, but I keep getting glimpses of fuzzy pink slippers."

"Some child dropped its cotton candy. Now the cheerleaders look a lot better than the drill team, don't you think?" She turned to Inez to discuss Inez's sister Julianne's talents in comparison to the mere distaff mortals dressed in crotch-length skirts and sweaters that would leave indentation in their flesh.

I stood up and tried to peer over heads at the other side of the street. Miss Parchester wasn't tall enough to tower over anyone out of elementary school; I was going to have to rely on the fuzzies on the sidewalk. There was a flash of plastic on a head, and perhaps the point of a furled umbrella. Very promising, I told myself as I began to push through the crowd and find a way to cross the street. All I had to do was grab the fugitive, drag her away for a quiet chat, and assure her that she was no longer suspected of embezzlement. Or murder—for the most part.

At this point, with my toe in the gutter, the full regalia of the Farberville High School Marching Falconnettes took over the pavement. Brass horns, tubas, clarinets, drums—the whole shlemiel right out of River City, and it started with a *P* and rhymed with *T* and basically translated into serious blockade problems.

I was hopping up and down, trying to see over a sea of plumed hats and tuba bells, when I felt a hand on my shoulder. It started with a *P* and stood for Peter, as in Rosen.

"Are you looking for a potty?" he asked politely. "There's one in the drugstore behind us, and I think it's free. If not, I'll be glad to loan you a dime."

"That's not funny."

"But you are, with this imitation of a human pogo stick." He gave me a look that forbode all sorts of problems. "What's going on, Claire? You're not the sort to be possessed by demons, nor are you one to make a spectacle of yourself—without cause. You're behaving manically, and you must have a reason."

I will admit that I should have told him about the pink fuzzies. I was the one who had concluded that confession was good for the soul, if not the ego, and that I would jeopardize the relationship if I continued to hide things from him. But I wanted to talk to Miss Parchester, and I wanted to do it alone. Okay, I wanted to do it first. She would be thoroughly spooked by a cop. I needed to calm her down, reassure her that the Judge's reputation was as safe as her own, and convince her she could come back to school—in time to chaperone the dance.

It would mean a great deal to her, this opportunity to show the students that she was, as always, above reproach. Having justified myself to myself, I gave Peter what I hoped was an enigmatic smile.

"I thought I saw an old classmate across the street, but the band cut me off at the pass. It's not important; I'll probably run into her some other time. Why don't you come sit with Caron, Inez, and me?"

The flower box proved adequate for four bottoms. The band finally passed on, in the literal sense, and was replaced by the senior float, "Bye-bye, Bantams." The girls looked rather nervous, sensing competition from the upper classmen, but they managed a few catty comments about the unevenness of the lettering on the banner.

Peter gave me a wry smile and put his hand over mine, just as if I weren't a treacherous, conniving, faithless quisling. He looked startled at my sigh, but I could only shake my head and look away as I tried to convince myself, as Caron would say, to Do The Right Thing.

As the moral dilemma raged, Jorgeson came over. "We lost her, Lieutenant. We spotted her in that jam of people across the street, and tried to sort of surround her without her noticing, but it didn't work so well. That dame can scamper like a frightened puppy, and the uniformed officer couldn't bring himself to tackle someone who resembles his grandmother. Said it was too cruel."

Peter glanced at me, then stood up and pulled Jorgeson a few steps away. "Does the uniformed officer with the unsullied conscience realize this woman is wanted in a murder investigation, that she may well have poisoned two people in the last eight days?" he said loudly enough to be heard over "Flaunt Thy Feathers, Falcons" or whatever. "Tell him to report to me in one hour. Now, alert all the patrol cars to watch for her on the sidewalk in at least a six-block radius."

Jorgeson saluted with one finger and hurried away to do as ordered, the back of his neck noticeably red against his navy jacket. Peter sat down next to me, harrumphed under his breath like an asthmatic whale, and stared fiercely at the rows of boy scouts straggling in front of us.

"Will you still take me dancing?" I asked.

A series of harrumphs ensued, punctuated with sighs and dark looks from under a lowered brow. "I have to coordinate a dragnet all over the damn town tonight. Beat the bushes. Search dumpsters. Find a suspect who has once again eluded us, although it seems she might have been apprehended had we been given a discreet tip."

"The dance doesn't start until ten-thirty."

"Perhaps you can persuade your old classmate to go with you."

"The sight of policemen was likely to frighten her, and she needed to be approached by a friendly, familiar face. I was going to convince her to turn herself in at the station."

"Class of what?"

"Nineteen aught three. We rode dinosaurs to school, wrote in cuneiform, and eagerly awaited the invention of the jitterbug."

"Well, tonight you'll have a wonderful chance to jitterbug till dawn. I will be occupied at headquarters those same hours, bawling out the uniformed officer and eagerly awaiting the apprehension of Miss Emily Parchester."

The conversation was clearly going nowhere, and I was clearly going to chaperone the Homecoming dance alone. I was saved from further remarks by the appearance of "Broast the Bantams," accompanied by hordes of goose-stepping freshmen yelling unintelligible things about the future of the freshmen, class of '90. They seemed to be predicting they would do "mighty finey."

"That doesn't rhyme," I pointed out to Caron once she and Inez had ceased their shrieks.

"Nothing ryhmes with 'ninety,'" she said. "We had to come up with something to yell at pep rallies and this sort of thing, but no one could produce a single acceptable rhyme."

"I'll have to agree with that. Who thought up 'mighty finey'?"

"I did, Mother."

Peter glowered from one side of me, Caron from the other. Miss Dort was undoubtedly displeased with me, as was a nameless pregnant woman, the denizens of the lounge, a paranoic Parchester, and the staff of Happy Meadows.

I told Caron and Inez to find a ride home, gave Peter a shrug, and exited to my bookstore, where there were no storms in the port. The jackhammer provide a pleasant drone that precluded thought. It was exactly what I needed.

"E" "L" "E" "V" "E" "N"

The Book Depot grew dim as the day latened, but I did not turn on a light in the front room. The street crew had departed in a roar of dozers and dump trucks, and the ensuing tranquillity was too lovely to be disrupted. I waltzed about with a feather duster, savoring the solitude as I sneezed my way through a week's accumulation of dust. The teachers' lounge seemed very distant; naggish thoughts of the dance were firmly dismissed.

I was in my office at the back, nose-deep in a ledger that appeared to have been depleted by an embezzler, but in reality was depressingly self-depleted, when I heard someone knock on the door. Despite the "closed" sign, customers did occasionally insist on admittance. One would think *they* could read.

It was Evelyn, her cheeks flushed from the chill in the air and her eyes bright from, I supposed, the excitement of the parade. I let her in and invited her to the office for coffee.

"No thanks," she said, "we're going to have to hurry if we're going to be on time for the game. Because of the Homecoming activities, it begins half an hour earlier than usual, and the bleachers are apt to be packed."

"Is this some kind of cruel joke?"

She shook her head. I protested steadily as I turned off the office light and locked the door. I continued to protest as I was driven to my apartment to fetch a scarf, hat, and gloves; and I did not falter as I ate a hamburger, drank several gallons of coffee as a preventive measure against the cold night air, and actually paid money to a gate attendent to be admitted to Falcon Stadium, Home of the Fighting Falcons, No Alcoholic Beverages Permitted. At that point, my protests became not only redundant, but also irrelevant.

We joined Sherwood on the fifty-yard line. A red-and-gold plaid blanket awaited us, along with a thermos of coffee and a discreet flask of brandy. I had not attended a football game since high school, having managed to avoid them throughout college as a matter of principle. Scrunched between Evelyn and Sherwood, my feet already numbing, my nose beginning to drip, surrounded on four sides by screaming fans, I remembered why.

"Why did you do this to me?" I asked Evelyn. "I was having a perfectly nice time at the Book Depot. I planned to go home, read the newspaper over a Lean Cuisine and a drink, and prepare myself for the dance. My plans did not include freezing in the bleachers, spilling coffee in my lap, or watching a group of faceless hulks batter each other to pulp over an ovoid plaything."

Evelyn laughed. "But it's Homecoming, Claire. We must applaud the ladies of the court and cheer on the Falcons to victory. Where's your school spirit?"

"In my living room, curled on the couch."

"Try this," Sherwood murmured, handing me a liberally spiked cup of coffee. "It's my contribution to spirit. Enough of this and you'll be on your feet with the *optimates* screeching for a touchdown."

"I thought this was forbidden," I said. I sipped at it anyway; the worst they could do was haul me away to jail, which was probably a good deal warmer and quieter.

"*De minimis non curat lex;* the law does not concern itself with trifles, such as a dollop of brandy." He prepared cups for Evelyn and himself. "I heard an interesting tidbit from my fifth period *hoi polloi,* by the way. It seems that Immerson was reinstated at the fateful moment, and the Falcons now have a chance to broast, barbecue, and bake the Bantams."

"That's odd," Evelyn said. "He surely didn't produce a grade above a *D* on a pop quiz or turn in an assignment in his own handwriting. Word of that would have spread across the school more quickly than a social disease. Did Miss Dort actually relent and agree to let him play?"

"All I heard was that our Mr. Immerman was in the office most of third period," Sherwood said, "and Jerry was there during fourth period. His absence encouraged the drivers' ed class to engage in a brief but successful game of strip poker in the backseat of the Buick; an anonymous young lady was rumored to have lost *a capite ad calcem*—from head to heel." He waggled his eyebrows in a facetious leer, but I didn't doubt the story for a second. "But there is our principal *pro tempore* a mere dozen rows away; you might ask her why she changed the policy. Personally, I would rather consult Medusa about the name of her hairdresser."

I agreed with Sherwood, although I was curious. I finished my coffee and asked for directions to the concession stand. Once we had unwrapped the blanket, much as the Egyptians might have done to check on decomposition, I fought my way down the rows of metal benches and went to see if Jerry had confided the details to his beloved.

Paula Hart was in the back of the concrete shed, watching popcorn explode in a glass box. I inched my way through the crowd to a corner of the counter and beckoned to her. "I hear Immerman was reinstated," I said.

She gave me a puzzled look. "Yes, I believe he was. Can I get you a box of popcorn or something to drink, Claire? We have a limited selection of candy bars, but they're ancient and I wouldn't recommend them to anyone over eighteen."

"Did he convince Miss Dort to rescind the order, or did Jerry have a word with her?"

A frown that hinted of irritation flashed across her face, but she quickly converted it to a smile. "I have no idea. It's really too loud and crazy in here for conversation, and I do have to watch some of the less mathematically inclined when they make change. Perhaps you might ask Miss Dort."

"I'd love a box of popcorn," I said, determined not to be dismissed despite the jostling crowd and my disinclination to eat anything prepared by adolescents. When she returned, I began to dig through my purse. "Now that Miss Dort is acting principal, what do you think she'll do about Jerry's graduate-school transcript?"

Paula's hand tightened around the box until I could almost hear the popcorn groan. "I have no idea what you're talking about," she managed to say, her lipstick beginning to crack.

"I'd ask him, but I suspect he'll be occupied with this thing between the Falcons and the Bantams for the next two hours. Of course, it wasn't clear what Mr. Weiss intended to do. He sounded grim at the last teachers' meeting, however; you two must have been alarmed." The last bit wasn't exactly speculation, but it seemed tactful to pretend.

"The police haven't mentioned the graduate-school transcripts. How did you find out about them?"

"The police have the same problem I had initially," I said. "They saw them in the personnel file, but they didn't assume there was anything significant about the coach being exceptionally well educated. One has to understand the workings of the education bureaucracy to see why all teachers shouldn't be exceptionally well educated."

Her Barbie doll face crumpled. Ignoring the startled looks from the students beside her, she snatched up a napkin and blotted her eyes. "It was awful, just awful. Weiss made it clear he could have Jerry fired at any time. He also stopped me in the corridor late one afternoon after a club meeting and suggested that he—he and I engage in—in—a—oh, it was dreadful!"

"Did you tell Jerry that Weiss wanted sexual favors in exchange for job security?" I continued, unmoved by her display.

"Jerry called me that evening, and I just broke down." She sniffled bravely into the napkin. "He was furious, but I managed to calm him down and talk some sense into him. He wanted to go right over to Mr. Weiss's house, pound on the door, and make a terrible scene. It would have cost him his job for sure. With that on his record, he wouldn't have been able to coach anywhere."

Or buy a cottage and reproduce, I amended to myself. I was about to ask more questions when the bleachers above us erupted in a roar. The band took up the strains of the Falcons' fight song, competing with the opposing band's blare. Paula gave me an apologetic look and scurried away to blink bravely, if somewhat damply, at the popcorn machine. I left the crushed box of cold popcorn on the counter, and went back to join Sherwood and Evelyn on the fifty-yard line.

The band marched onto the field and arranged itself in some mysterious way that must have had some significance to those higher in the tiers. The cheerleaders bounced about like irregular pingpong balls, shaking their pompoms among other things and arousing the pep squad to frenzied squeals. The drill team formed two lines and shook their pompoms among other things. The scene reminded me of a primitive, sacrificial ceremony in which virgins would go to the grave intact. To the tune of "Fight Ye Falcons," no less. The crowd loved it.

The Homecoming court convertibles appeared on the track that encircled the football field. The girls perched on the backseats, their white, clenched fingers digging into the upholstery as they smiled at the crowd. They were escorted from their thrones by as-yet-unsullied football players to be presented to the crowd and to accept bouquets and admiration. Followed by the kindergarten attendants, Cheryl Anne clutched the arm of her darling Thud, who clumsily put a plastic tiara on her head and handed her a bouquet of roses. It brought back memories, distant and blessedly mellowed with time, of faces arranged in the yearbook, all grim and determined to succeed. I looked particularly stern under a bouffant hairstyle that always left Caron and Inez weak from sustained laughter.

The presentation of the court, sniveling babes and all, was touching. The next two-and-a-half hours of bodies flinging themselves against each other were not, except in the obvious sense. Grunts and thumps, the sound of helmet against helmet, the incessant screams of the pep squad, the boisterous verbosity of the fans—it verged on something worse than Dante had ever envisioned for the lowest circles of the *Inferno*.

The thermos ran dry. The flask went the same way. My feet forsook me and my hands turned blue. My nose ran a marathon. I was kicked from behind and elbowed from both sides. A coke dribbled down my neck during a particularly exciting play.

The majority of the plays were incomprehensible, although I did my best to follow both the ball and the seesaw score. The home team took the lead, then lost it via a fumble. Thud snatched the ball from a Bantam and scampered all the way to the goal line, sending the cheerleaders into paroxysms of glee. The Bantams doggedly scored once again. Everyone in the bleachers, with one exception, rose and fell with pistonish precision.

The final quarter arrived, along with a couple of Falcon fumbles and Bantam triumphs, causing the scoreboard to tilt dangerously to the enemy side. Just as I neared a frostbite-induced coma, the referees called it a night. The cheerleaders burst into tears on each other's shoulders, while the band played a version of the fight song that seemed more of a dirge. Cheryl Anne stalked down from the bleachers, paused to hiss at the forlorn Falcons, then led her cortege into the metaphorical sunset. Thud threw his helmet on the ground, having displayed enough fore-sight to remove his head from it first. The coaches shook hands and trudged across the field, their troops in straggly formation behind them.

"Shall we go?" I said, trying not to sound too heartened by the thought of a car heater and even a gymnasium.

Evelyn sighed. "It's such a shame to lose the Homecoming game. The kids really care about this sort of thing."

"Absolutely," I said. "Shall I carry the blanket? Where's the nearest exit?"

Sherwood glanced at me, but offered no editorial. We fol-lowed the stream out of the stadium. The students punched each other on the shoulder and verbally rehashed the final plays of the game; their liberal use of profanity was more than mildly disturb-ing to someone who would be obliged to restrain them in the immediate future.

I tugged at Evelyn's arm. "What precisely is my assignment at the dance?"

"You have floor duty. Emily always volunteered for it, swear-ing she enjoyed it, and no one ever argued with her for the privilege." Her voice dropped until it was almost inaudible. "You'll survive, probably."

"Floor duty?" I said.

Sherwood patted me on the shoulder. "You are the ultimate *in loco parentis,* dear sleuth. All you must do is keep the rabble from dancing too closely together—school policy is three inches and not a whit closer—and the ones sitting down to keep their paws off each other."

"And the band from singing obscenities," Evelyn added. "The lyrics can get pretty raunchy if you don't keep an eye on them."

"Don't let anyone drink anything that comes from a back pocket," said Sherwood. "No smoking, snuff, or chewing to-bacco. No vodka in the punchbowl. No fistfights. Don't let the girls roll up their skirts or the boys unzip their jeans."

"That's all?" I laughed gaily. "And I'm going to do this all by myself, right? I won't have a squadron of marines to help me out, or even an automatic weapon. I'll just shake my finger at perpetrators, and they'll back off from whatever felonious activity they've chosen."

"Oh, you'll have help." Evelyn gave me a wry look. "I believe you're assigned with Mr. Chippendale and Mr. Eugenia."

"Wonderful," I sighed. And I had alienated Peter, whose presence might have saved me from what threatened to be slightly worse than root-canal surgery done by a drunken dentist—in a bouncing jeep. Just when I needed a whiff of nitrous oxide.

Evelyn drove us to the faculty lot. We went to the gym, which was dripping with red-and-gold crepe paper, and glumly surveyed the battlefield. I presumed it would be strewn with bodies by midnight; all I could hope was that mine would not be included in the count.

Speakers the size of refrigerators were arranged in front of a low platform cluttered with beglittered guitars and an intricate formation of drums. The acned boys in the band huddled on one side, their eyes darting as if they anticipated attack or arrest. They had long, stringy hair and feral expressions. A droopy banner taped on the wall above them proclaimed them to be "Pout," an ominously appropriate name. Evelyn and Sherwood wished me luck, then drifted away to their assigned posts elsewhere in the building, where they might not even be able to hear Pout's best efforts to deafen us.

Mr. Chippendale came through the door, metal chairs under his arms. "Ah, yes, Mrs. Malloy, are you prepared for the dance?"

"Certainly, Mr. Chippendale. I've made a new will, consulted a neurologist about potential auditory nerve damage, and booked a private room at Happy Meadows."

He gave me a startled look, then busied himself unfolding chairs along the wall. A grayish man with bifocals introduced himself as Erwin "Gene" Eugenia, Algebra and Trig, and took a stack of chairs to the opposite side of the vast room. Students drifted in to set up the refreshment table, all sober from the defeat at the hands (talons?) of the Starley City Bantams. I watched them carry in the punch bowl, reminding myself that I was assigned the formidable task of assuring their continued sobriety until the dance was done.

A short while later the gym began to swell with students. After a few false starts, Pout found its stride and broke into what was presumably their opening set. Mr. Chippendale took a post next to the stage, although I doubted he could isolate stray obscenities in the ululation that passed as lyrics. Mr. Eugenia stayed beside the punch bowl, leaving me to monitor the dancers for distance and the nondancers for discretion.

Once my ears grew accustomed to the volume, I realized I might survive. Some of the students from the journalism classes spoke to me, or at least moved their mouths in what I interpreted as amiable discourse. I smiled politely, though blankly. No one asked me to dance, which was for the best since I had had no training in that particular mode of stylized warfare.

During a lull, I spotted Caron and Inez near the door. For the first time since the onslaught of puberty, my daughter looked timid and vulnerable; Inez appeared to be in the early stages of a seizure. After a beady look at a leather-clad hoodlum with an earring and fast hands, I joined them. "I didn't see you two at the game."

Caron regained some of her usual superciliousness. "You went to the football game, Mother? Whatever for?"

"I was coerced," I admitted. "I sat with Mrs. West and Mr. Timmons in what I fear was the most vocal section of the bleachers. I suppose it was good practice for the decibel level in here."

"Caron and I sold programs at the south gate," Inez volunteered. "We turned in our money, then sat with Rhonda and some of the girls. Wasn't the game just dreadful?"

"I thought so," I said, suspecting our criteria were different. Pout roared into song once again; conversation was impossible. Caron grabbed Inez's shoulder, and they hobbled away to find seats amidst the wallflowers.

Despite the lack of a victory, the kids seemed to be enjoying themselves. I was beginning to feel somewhat confident when Cheryl Anne swept through the door and stopped to survey the scene, her mouth a tight red rosebud and her hands clenched at her sides. Thud hovered behind her, clearly uncomfortable in her wake.

The dancers nearest the door halted in mid-gyration and backed off the floor to make a path that would have led straight to the throne, had there been one. I was mildly surprised no one had thought to bring a red carpet.

Cheryl Anne snapped her fingers over her shoulder. "Don't just stand there, for God's sake. I want to dance."

Thud's eyes were almost invisible under his lowered brow, but he lumbered around her to his designated spot. "Come on, then—dance, damn it," he grunted. After a second of icy disdain, Cheryl Anne joined him and they disappeared into the mass of writhing bodies. I was not the only wallflower to let out my breath, Tupperwear-style.

At the end of the second set, the lead guitarist announced they were "gonna haf to break" for fifteen minutes so their "instruments could like cool off, you know." I slipped out the door to assess whether I had brain damage, and promptly bumped into my Baker Street Irregulars.

"I saw Miss Parchester!" Caron said, her fingers digging into my arm. "She's in the building."

"When did you see her, and where is she?"

"We saw her go around a corner when we went to hide in the rest room," Inez said.

"Hide in the rest room?" I said, momentarily distracted.

"The geek, Mother. He's here—and he keeps looking at me,"

Caron said. "Anyway, we tried to catch Miss Parchester, but we couldn't keep up with her. My ankle, you know."

"I know," I said. "Tell Mr. Chippendale that I've gone to the lounge for an aspirin, and that I'll be back after the break. Miss Parchester probably went to the basement to look for clues or some such thing. Perhaps I can persuade her to listen to me."

I headed for the basement, aware that I was spending an inordinate amount of time in the dark bowels of this building. My flashlight was still in my purse (I do profit from experience), and I switched it on as I scuttled down the stairs. The corridor was empty. The lounge was locked. The journalism room was dark and still and held no hidden presence that I could discern from the doorway.

As I paused under the exit light to think, I noticed one of the classroom doors was ajar. A taped card had Miss Zuckerman's name and a list of classes, which included such esoteric things as Steno II and A-V Machines: Advanced. Miss Parchester might have slipped in to pick up something for her friend, I decided as I eased through the door.

If she had, she was already gone. I shined the light on the far wall, which had inspirational messages taped in a tidy row. "Clean ribbons make clear copies." "Type right on your typewriter." The back wall exhorted the students to practice their swirls and curlicues. "Shorthand—your key to a good job." A travel poster that touted the charms of Juarez contributed the one splash of color in an otherwise drab decor. Miss Zuckerman must have felt quite naughty when she included it, I thought with a sigh. "Nimble fingers come from practice." My light continued around the room. "Join the Future Secretaries of America." "Speed and spelling equal salary."

I decided to search the room in case Miss Parchester had inadvertently dropped some vital clue, such as a motel key. I began with the rows of shrouded typewriters and worked my way to the desk drawers. I expected to find rosters and lesson plans. I did not expect to find a crude little cigarette in an envelope.

During the sixties, I had encountered such things, sometimes in an intimate fashion. That had been more than fifteen years ago, however, and I was not sure I could trust my aged nose to ascertain if this was truly a marijuana cigarette. It seemed absurd that Tessa Zuckerman would have one stashed in her desk; she was hardly my idea of a dope dealer.

I could have called the police station and told Peter about my discovery. He could have sent Jorgeson over to collect the evidence and deliver it to the lab to be tested. Then he could have arranged for Miss Zuckerman to be transferred to a cell next to Miss Parchester's, so that the two little old ladies could chat as they withered away in their prison garb. A murderer and a dope dealer, both with silver hair and porcelain skin. . . .

I took a book of matches from my purse and lit the thing. If it turned out to be some thug's innocent attempt to save a few cents on prefabricated cigarettes, then there would be no reason not to drop it in the trash can and go about my business. If it was illegally potent, I would have to tell Peter—at some point. I inhaled deeply and waited for the answer.

Oddly enough, I thought I could see Peter's face. I was sitting on the floor, my head against the desk, when the light came on overhead and footsteps echoed like a Poutian revival. Frowning, I squinted up at the face hovering above me. No body, mind you. It was very, very peculiar. I warned myself to watch out.

"Claire?" it actually said. It sounded like Peter's voice, which struck me as highly amusing, if not outright uproarious.

I clamped my hand over my giggle—my mouth—and said, "Where's the rest of you?"

The rest of him came around the desk and squatted in front of me. "What's wrong with you, Claire? Why are you sitting on the floor in a dark classroom?" His nose wrinkled (quite adorably, I thought), and he looked at the smoldering butt in my hand.

"Where did you get a joint, for Christ's sake—and why are you smoking it now? Here?"

"Don't have time later," I told him smugly. "I'm in charge of five hundred—count 'em—five hundred juvenile delinquents who want to dance all over each other. Want to show 'em how to jitterbug, Supercop?"

"You are stoned," he said in a stunned voice. "I presume there's an explanation for this, and that you're going to give it to me. Right?"

"I am not stoned. I am merely conducting an experiment, like the one I did with the pit peach. Peach pit. Remember when you saw me on the sidewalk with the hammer? It must have looked really funny." I started to laugh as I recalled his expression, then discovered I was helpless to stop—but I didn't mind one teeny-weeny bit. Finally I got hold of myself, or of something. It may have been Peter's shoe.

"Give me the joint." He held out his hand, and I obediently handed over the remains. He pulled me to my feet, which seemed to belong to someone else, and steadied me. "We are going to the lounge for a nice pot of coffee. I have a feeling you're not quite ready to return to the dance."

"I am too ready," I sniffed. "A little wobbly, perhaps, but more than capable of chaperonage. I may even dance, if anyone asks me. Maybe by myself. Anyway, the lounge is locked. We can't get in because we don't have a key. Not even Supercop can walk through doors that are locked. Will you dance with me?"

He mutely showed me a key, then propelled me down the hall and into the lounge. I was placed unceremoniously on the mauve monster, and informed that I was not to move while he made coffee. Which was dandy with me, since I wasn't sure I could move in any case. In any direction.

"If you want to arrest me, go ahead. I was chasing Miss Parchester," I informed the doorway of the kitchenette, "and I lost her again. That woman is as fast as a damn minnow, and as slippery as a damn sardine. We ought to stake out the public aquarium, Peter."

He came back into the room and handed me a cup of coffee. "I saw Caron in the gym, and she told me you were in hot pursuit of Miss Parchester."

"For the zillionth time," I agreed. "I thought you were on a stakeout, Sherlock. What are you doing at the school?"

"I came to check on you. You are, shall we say, at times unconventional in your investigative techniques."

"Unconventional?" That rang a bell somewhere, but all I could do was blink at him. Bravely, I hoped.

"As in overzealous, impetuous, and illegal," he said, holding the last of the joint in his fingertips.

I couldn't tell if his smile was sincere or sarcastic, but I did like the color of his eyes. When I said as much, he pointed at the coffee cup and turned just a tad pink. "This isn't my cup," I said, studying the intricate swirls of roses and pastel leaves. "This could warrant a firing squad—or worse, you know. After you finish locking up poor Miss Parchester and poor Miss Zuckerman, will you come to my funeral?"

"Miss Parchester is still at large, and Miss Zuckerman is tucked safely in her hospital bed. As for the funeral, I'll make a point of attending—it will be the one time I know exactly where you are and what you're doing."

I didn't much like that, but I decided to let it go. "Mrs. Platchett takes this cup thing pretty seriously. She was more upset at me for borrowing her cup than she was about the deviled eggs."

"Why was she upset about the deviled eggs?" he asked, not sounding especially concerned about my welfare.

"Well, she wasn't upset about the deviled eggs, because Pitts hadn't poked them. Did you know that broccoli doesn't take fingerprints?"

"Actually, it does, but we can discuss the technical aspects later. Why did she think Pitts might poke the deviled eggs?"

"He poked everything." I rubbed my forehead, which was beginning to ache. "I think I'd better have some more coffee."

"I think you may recover," he said with a smile. "Will you please tell me why I stumbled on to a stoned bookseller in the basement of the high school?"

I told him why. We agreed that I had erred in my decision to test the contents of the cigarette, and that I should have called him. I drank more coffee, my head propped on his shoulder, and told him about the problem of Jerry's transcript, Paula's reaction, and Thud Immerman's reinstatement. None of it amazed him, although he did seem interested.

"Paula's not as sweet as she acts," I said, snuggling into his chest. "She might have murdered Weiss to protect her future, or she might have persuaded Jerry to do the dirty deed in order to protect her virtue."

"He wasn't in the lounge, and neither was she."

"The murderer did have to enter the lounge between ten and ten-fifteen, when Evelyn came in to use the ladies room." I glanced at the closed door of said establishment. "If I'd known about the hole, I might have murdered Pitts myself."

"The hole was discovered the day after Weiss's funeral, so it could have been a motive in the second murder. We just can't find a decent motive for Weiss's murder, except vengeance."

"Meaning Miss Parchester?"

"I'm sorry, Claire. I don't enjoy the idea of chasing some elderly lady around Farberville to question her about her recipe for peach compote, but she did have a reason to be angry at Weiss. I do need to ask her a few questions, if only to permit her to prove her innocence."

"I know," I said, sighing. The fuzzy pink slippers must have been wearing thin, considering the miles they'd done in the last

six days. The hospital, the parade, the dance, probably the football game, and the school. The woman had been everywhere, but
was nowhere to be found—while the Judge rotated in his grave.
"What are you going to do about the marijuana in Miss Zuckerman's desk?"

"Ask her, although I would imagine she confiscated it from
one of her students."

"And failed to turn it in to the authorities? If she's like her
sister Furies, she's probably a stickler for regulations. Maybe she
found it the day of the potluck and did not have an opportunity
to deal with it."

He nodded. Before he could say anything, Caron limped into
the lounge. "Mr. Chippendale is frantic, Mother. He sent me to
search for you, because the band members took off their shirts
and he thinks they may take off more. He says they are virtually
Out of Control, although I don't know what he expects you to
do."

"Call in the cavalry," I said, smiling at Peter. "Surely you can
strike a chord of fear in their atonal souls."

We went to the gym. We didn't, however, jitterbug until
dawn. Actually, it was more like three in the morning.

"T·W·E·L·V·E"

I went the Book Depot the next morning and opened up for business, the ledgers having hinted at the desirability of earning a few dollars, if not an actual fistful or more. I sold books, straightened shelves, filed invoices, and griped long-distance about delayed orders. It was all fairly normal until Caron and Inez limped through the door, gasping and panting. As always, normalcy fled in the face of postpubescent theatrics. I could not.

"Did you hear about Cheryl Anne and Thud?" Caron demanded.

"No, I heard about a fire at a university press and something about an order shipped to Alaska by mistake, but nary a word about the queen and the jock."

"They Broke Up." Caron folded her arms and stared at me, willing me to blanche, grab the edge of the counter, and beg for further details. "They've been going steady for Two Whole Years," she added when preliminary fireworks failed to explode.

"A blessing for the future of the human race," I said. "I cringe at the thought of the offspring those two might have conceived."

Inez gulped. "It was terrible, Mrs. Malloy. They had a big scene in the parking lot after the dance, and Cheryl Anne told Thud to drop dead, preferably in the middle of the highway."

"In front of a truck," Caron added.

"He was furious." Inez.

"He called her dreadful names." Caron.

"Slut." Inez, with a shiver.

"Cheap little whore." Caron, without.

"She told him he was a miserable football player, that he ought to play against twelve-year-old girls." Inez.

"He said he'd played with little girls too long." Caron.

"He said he was ready for a real woman." Inez.

The Abbott and Costello routine was giving me a pain in the neck, physically as well as metaphorically. I held up my hand and said, "Wait a minute, please. I really am not interested in an instant replay of their witticisms, no matter how colorful they may have been. May I assume Cheryl Anne was upset because Thud failed to win the game single-handedly and ensure a Homecoming celebration fraught with significance and glistening memories?"

Caron and Inez nodded, enthralled by my perspicacity.

"And," I continued, "she was especially upset because she had worked so hard to see that he was eligible to play?" More nods. "By the way, how did Thud convince Miss Dort to reinstate him?"

"Nobody knows," Caron said, widening her eyes to convey the depth of her bewilderment. I wasn't sure if it came from the inexplicable behavior of her elders or the failure of the grapevine to ascertain the gory details.

"It's sheer mystery," Inez said. She attempted the same ploy, but she looked more like an inflated puffer fish. She needed practice. And perhaps contact lenses.

I shooed them out the door and sat down behind the counter. There were too many unanswered questions driting around the corridors of Farberville High School, too many petty schemes and undercurrents. Too many bits of conversation that might—or might not—have relevance. Way too much gossip.

I called Evelyn, my primary source of gossip. "Who has a key to the building?" I asked once we'd completed the necessary pleasantries.

"Very few," she told me. "Mr. Weiss decided several years ago that loose keys sank ships, or something to that effect. All of the teachers were required to turn in their keys."

"Sherwood has one."

"Sherwood lives next door to a locksmith. His copy is illicit, but it's saved both of us a lot of hassle when we've forgotten a stack of tests or one of the dreaded must-have-first-thing-in-the-morning forms."

"Have you heard of anyone else with a copy?"

"No," she said after some thought. "Weiss had one, naturally, as did Bernice. Perhaps school board members, although I don't know why. Head of maintenance, but no one on the level of Pitts."

"Miss Parchester or the Furies?" I said without much hope.

"Of course not. None of the teachers except an anomaly like Sherwood would want to have an illicit copy of the key. If something happened in the building after school hours, I certainly would like to be able to swear, under oath or polygraph, that I didn't have access."

"You're fond of the anomaly, aren't you?"

"I suppose I am." The confession sounded sad.

I told her that there'd been someone in the building the night Sherwood and I had indulged in a mild spot of prowling. She was fairly sure it couldn't have been a teacher—unless it was the one who'd let me in the building in the first place. I was fairly sure Sherwood hadn't stolen the letters from under my nose. I asked her if she'd heard anything further about the mysterious reinstatement of the jock, and she told me that she hadn't.

I bade her farewell, took a deep breath, and called Miss Bernice Dort. After eleven unanswered rings, I hung up in disgust.

When Peter wandered by later in the morning, I was still behind the counter, staring at the nonfiction shelves and grumbling under my breath. "Any progress?" I asked morosely.

"Miss Parchester continues to elude us, and she seems to be

our only decent suspect thus far. The lab reports are back, but they don't say much of anything we hadn't already suspected. Pitts ingested more than three hundred fifty milligrams of cyanide, which was dissolved in the whiskey."

"Was it also organic?"

"It was. A sample has been sent to the regional lab for a more precise analysis, but it'll take weeks to get the results. We're presuming Pitts was murdered with—well, with pits."

"Pitts poked the peach pits. . . ." I said, gnawing on my lip.

Peter grinned. "That's what you claimed last night, among other more whimsical things."

"There are too many damn p's in this. Pitts the peeper, peaches, Parchester, plagiarism, Paula, principals, pouters, poisonous pits, and parades! It's worse than the jackhammer."

"Not to mention policemen and prowling prevaricators."

"Stop the p's!" I gestured for him to accompany me to my office, where I offered (not poured) coffee and a dusty chair. "I am going to figure this damn thing out without any further alliteration. Let's begin with another source for the toxic substance."

"It's definitely organic," Peter said, leaning back with a tolerant expression. "Officers of the law do not dismiss coincidences; they leap on them. Toxic compote, made from . . . a certain fruit with a toxic interior."

"But Jorgeson told me that cyanide is found in the seeds of a variety of fruits. Apples, cherries, apricots, and so forth—why couldn't one of those be the source?"

"One of them could, I suppose, but we haven't come across any of them in the investigation."

I stared at him. "I may have, though."

He stared right back. "When? What?"

"It's just a wild guess—but there was a souvenir from Mexico."

"Lots of tourists go to Mexico, Claire; they all buy things to bring home and discard a few weeks later. Hundreds of thousands of tourists, I would estimate."

"And they go for a variety of reasons, both conventional and unconventional." I toyed with the theory for a few minutes, trying to find slots for all the disparate bits of information (not pieces of the puzzle, mind you). "Apricots and Mexico. The joint in the desk. Charles Dickens. It almost makes sense, Lieutenant Rosen, although it means we've been looking at this thing from the wrong side of the hole."

"Apricots, Mexico, Dickens, and dope? How many joints did you find in Miss Zuckerman's desk?"

"Just the one," I said distractedly. "It was evidence of a sort, although I don't think we'll need it for court. The murderer is going to get away with the crime. We couldn't see the apricots for the peaches."

"I'm not sure you've fully recovered from the effects of the marijuana," he said, looking at me as if I were atop the file cabinet with a rose clenched between my teeth. "We might run by the hospital and have you checked for lingering euphoria."

"My idea, exactly." I grabbed my jacket and hurried out of the office, followed by a bewildered cop (as opposed to a perplexed policeman). I directed him to drive me to the hospital, then clammed up and stared out the window.

As we neared the lot, I told him that I wanted to visit Miss Zuckerman before he arranged for a straitjacket and a handful of Thorazine. When he sputtered, I suggested we question her about the joint that was ingested in the name of scientific discovery. He agreed, albeit with minimal grace.

I stopped at the nurses' station to inquire about Miss Zuckerman's status. We were informed that she was critical, but allowed short visits by close friends and family members. She did look critical, more frail than she'd been a few days ago and even

grayer. Her skin was translucent, her bruised arms sprouting needles and tubes that led to bags above her head.

She managed a smile. "Mrs. Malloy, how kind of you."

"I believe you know Lieutenant Rosen," I murmured. "We
stopped by for only a minute, so please let us know when you're
too tired for visitors."

"I intend to enjoy my visitors as long as I'm here," she said.
"This morning Alexandria and Mae came by to tell me about the
Homecoming game. So hard for the students to lose their big
game, but they'll get over it. The resilience of youth in the face of
disaster is remarkable, you know, as long as they can rely on the
wisdom of their elders to protect them from true evil."

"Drug dealers, for instance?" I said softly.

"Wicked, wicked people."

"It must have been difficult to see Pitts every day when you
knew what dreadful things he was doing to the students."

"He was *very* wicked."

"The marijuana cigarette was the last straw, wasn't it?" I
prompted, ignoring Peter's sudden intake of breath behind me.

"I'd been observing him for several months, but this was the
first time I actually saw him sell drugs. The student, when confronted, was properly contrite and vowed to never again purchase
illegal substances, but I knew Pitts had to be removed from Farberville High School. Since Mr. Weiss seemed unwilling to take
action, I felt obliged to act on my convictions."

"You happened to have cyanide with you—in your purse, I
would guess—and you knew Pitts would eat anything that
caught his fancy in the refrigerator in the teachers' lounge."

She gave me a beatific smile. "Very good, dear. I'm not sure
that I intended to kill him; I hoped he would become very ill, and
perhaps quit his job and go elsewhere. I crushed a dozen or so
pills and mixed them in Emily's little jar of compote. I never
dreamed Mr. Weiss would eat it first . . . but he wasn't a very
nice man, either. He was supposed to set an example for the

students, yet he was having an affair with Bernice Dort. I was listening at my post when Pitts sold the information to Cheryl Anne, who seemed to be pleased to learn her father was a philanderer. I was appalled, I must say."

I felt an elbow in my back. I ground my heel on a convenient foot, then bent over the hospital bed and said, "No one saw you enter or leave the lounge, Miss Zuckerman."

"No one ever noticed me. After all those years, I'm afraid I simply became part of the backdrop, a pathetic gray ghost who haunted the basement of the school. Once I made up my mind to teach Pitts a lesson, I assigned a lengthy paragraph to my Ad Sten class, slipped off to the lounge, and returned without my absence being noticed."

"Was there anyone in the lounge?"

"Mrs. West's student teacher was present, but she didn't notice me, either. Young people tend to find the elderly invisible; it helps them avoid facing their own mortality." She glanced away for a moment. "It hasn't been a very exciting life, but it has been rewarding. I did take a trip to a foreign country once; it was dirty, yet the cultural differences intrigued me. I would have liked to travel more."

"The clinic in Mexico?"

"Yes, but the doctors there said it was too late to control the malignancy. I followed the diet and took the vitamins, enzymes, and tablets, hoping for a miracle. It did not occur. Now, if you don't mind, I think I'd better rest." Her eyelids drifted down with a faint flutter. She began to snore in a quiet, ladylike way.

Peter moved forward, but I caught his arm and pulled him out of the room. "Would you explain?" he snapped as we started for the elevator. "Am I correct in assuming Tessa Zuckerman murdered Weiss?"

"She did, although she was actually after Pitts. It was her farewell gift to the school."

"She 'happened' to have cyanide in her purse?"

"Laetrile, made from apricot pits. You remember the contro-versy about it in all the newspapers several years ago, don't you? The proponents claimed it was the ultimate cure for cancer; the medical authorities claimed it was quackery to exploit those poor souls too terrified to pass up any possibility. Ultimately, those who chose to try it had to go to clinics in Mexico, where it was legal."

"And Miss Zuckerman went to such an establishment, and brought home a supply of Laetrile tablets, along with a travel poster," Peter said. "When she decided to rid the school of its dope dealer, she crushed a few tablets and popped them in the compote?"

I nodded. "She made the hole in the women's rest room so that she could spy on Pitts to determine if he was indeed the villain he was rumored to be. He was telling the truth the day he claimed he hadn't made the hole, although I imagine that once he discovered it, he did use it to eavesdrop and report to Weiss. He lacked the acumen to realize that it could be used two ways."

"So Miss Zuckerman observed a transaction and decided to poison him," Peter said. "It didn't work out as she intended, although she did not seem inordinately disturbed by the result."

"Married men with families should not have affairs," I said, shrugging. "It might prove dangerous—or fatal."

"I'll note that in the report," he said. He rewarded me with a glimpse of his teeth. It was unsettling.

We drove back to my apartment. As we reached the top of the stairs, Caron hobbled out the door, caught sight of Peter, and froze in a posture reminiscent of Pout's lead guitarist in a mo-ment of spasmodic bliss.

"Oh," she breathed at us.

I tried to move around her, but she held her ground in the middle of the doorway. "You're supposed to go to the station," she said to Peter. "Right away, because of some emergency. They said to go right away."

"I'd better call in and see what's happening," he said.

"You don't have time to call. It's a terrible emergency, and they want you to hurry there without wasting any time on the telephone. Besides, Inez is talking to her sick grandmother in Nebraska."

He gave her a suspicious look, told me he'd call later, and left to face whatever dire trouble my Cassandra was so eager to predict. Once the front door closed below, said oracle stepped back and said, "Thank God we got rid of him, Mother. I wasn't prepared for him to be with you, and I couldn't think what to say."

"You made up that story? He'll learn the truth in about ten minutes, Caron, and he won't be amused." I went into the living room and stared at Inez, who was huddled in the corner with the telephone. "Why did Inez find a sudden compulsion to talk to her grandmother in Nebraska, for that matter? What on earth is—?"

"Miss Parchester," Inez whispered, pointing at the receiver. "Caron told me to keep her on the line until you got here, Mrs. Malloy. I think she's getting suspicious; you'd better take over now."

I grabbed the receiver. "Miss Parchester?"

"Mrs. Malloy, it's so lovely to have this opportunity to speak with you again after all this time. How are you?"

"I'm fine, Miss Parchester. Where are you?"

"I'm fine, thank you. I've seen you here and there, but it's been quite impossible to actually have a word in private. I seem to keep running into policemen wherever I go; it's so distressing."

"Where are you?" I repeated, determined to stay calm. "If you'll tell me where you are, I'll come right over and we can have many words in private. I have lots of things to tell you."

"I'd be delighted to have a little conference with you, since I realize you've worked hard on the investigation, but"—there was a long pause, during which I prayed she wasn't taking a discreet nip or two—"I do fear the presence of the police. They have been following me, and they may be following you, too. An undercover officer in a bizarre disguise literally attacked me at the hospital, but I was fortunate to elude him."

I was worried that Peter would storm up the stairs at any moment to discuss deception with my daughter. If I could only find Miss Parchester and allay her fears, then I knew I could persuade her to present herself at the police station. My track record wasn't very good, but I am an eternal optimist.

"Miss Parchester," I said with great earnestness, "I know who murdered Mr. Weiss. I know who fiddled with the journalism ledgers, and I know why. Don't you want me to come tell you about it?"

"I know all that, my dear," she giggled. "I'm a trained reporter, as you know, and I've been doing a little snooping. I feel incredibly akin to Miss Jane Marple. We're of a similar age."

As I gaped at the receiver, Caron tapped me on the shoulder. "Ask her if I can have an exclusive interview, Mother. We can put it on the front page of the *Falcon Crier,* with a byline, naturally, and maybe a photograph."

I made a face, took a breath, and searched my mind for the proper response to Miss Parchester's blithe assurance that she knew all that, my dear. My mind failed me. "You do?" I said.

"I've enjoyed our chat, Mrs. Malloy, but I'd better run along now," she said with the faintest hiccup. "I have an errand, and soon it will be teatime."

Before I could wiggle my jaw, the line went dead.

"You didn't even ask about the interview," Caron said, her lip inching forward in preparation for a scene. "Aren't you at all interested in my future in journalism?"

"I have a camera," Inez contributed sadly.

"You'd better worry about the immediate situation," I said as I headed for the liquor cabinet. "Once Peter returns, you may not have a future."

The girls discovered the necessity of retiring to the college library to work on reports for American history. I sank into the sofa and tried to find satisfaction in having identified Weiss's murderer, but it didn't leave me tingling with self-respect. Miss Zuckerman was too near death to be disturbed by the police; Peter would hide the report until she was gone, then file it away for posterity.

Miss Zuckerman had murdered Weiss, albeit in a haphazard manner. She had then been wheeled to the hospital, and had been incarcerated there ever since. Which led to an inescapable problem: Who poisoned Pitts? The memory of Miss Parchester's giggle began to haunt me. She seemed to be well informed of the identities of various players in the cast. Had she stumbled across the identity of the second murderer? Was she in danger?

She certainly couldn't defend herself with a fuzzy pink slipper. On the other hand, she had managed to avoid an entire police force for most of a week, so surely she could avoid a killer as well. If she wasn't one.

"She's innocent," I said, pounding the pillow. A lapse into alliteration, but justified. Where was she? I knew she wasn't at Mrs. Platchett's house, or at Miss Bagby's. She wasn't at home, the school, the police station, or the Book Depot (yes, I had looked). Peter had warned me that he had men at the hospital, but I decided she had enough of her wits left to avoid there. Happy Meadows would have turned her in like a shot, since "we" didn't want any problems with the police.

There was one place left, a fairly good possibility. I downed my scotch and hurried to my car, then hurried right back upstairs and grabbed the telephone book. The name was not listed. I hurried back downstairs, admittedly somewhat breathless by this time, and drove to Miss Bagby's duplex.

"I'm sorry to disrupt your weekend," I said when she appeared behind the screen, "but I need Tessa Zuckerman's address."

"She's still in the hospital, Mrs. Malloy."

"I was there earlier in the afternoon. I thought I might go by her house to water her plants and check on things," I said, not adding that the one thing I wanted to check on ran around town in bedroom slippers.

Miss Bagby had heard too many excuses about incomplete assignments and missing homework. "How remarkable of her to ask you rather than Alexandria or me," she said, her lips atwitch with doubt. "Did she give you a key?"

I considered telling her my dog ate it, but instead I said, "I walked right out of the hospital without it. She's doing poorly; I'd hate to disturb her about a minor detail like a house key, wouldn't you?"

After a moment of silence, Miss Bagby told me the address and the location of the house key, which was under the welcome mat. We're rather casual about that sort of thing in Farberville; it drives Peter Rosen et al crazy, but the burglars haven't caught on yet.

I drove to Miss Zuckerman's house and hid my car at the far end of the driveway. It was a tidy bungalow, similar to that of Mrs. Platchett—although I doubted a single leaf dared to fall on her yard. Here there were indications that no one had been home for several days. The shades were drawn, the door locked. The key was not under the welcome mat. Opting for simplicity, I rang the doorbell. Simplicity didn't work, so I sat down on the top step of the porch to consider my next move.

I was still sitting there, uninspired, when the pink fuzzies ambled up the sidewalk, with a few minor digressions to either side. Miss Parchester tried to pretend she hadn't noticed me, but I stood up, brushed off the seat of my pants, and trailed her into the house.

"It took me a long time to figure out where you were," I said. "I did accuse Mrs. Platchett and Miss Bagby of hiding you, but they were offended at the suggestion. I forgot to ask Tessa Zuckerman."

"She is a dear friend," Miss Parchester said. She took off her coat and plastic rain bonnet, propped her umbrella in a corner, and patted a few stray wisps of hair back into place. "She seemed slightly better today, although tired after her conversation with you and that nice policeman with whom you keep company."

"That nice policeman has been wanting a word with you for a week, as have I. In fact, that same policeman assigned several of his men to detain you, should you return to the hospital. Did you not encounter any of them?"

"I have been very cautious since I was attacked outside Tessa's room. Today I borrowed a bathrobe from a linen closet in order to pose as a patient; yesterday I wore a white coat and carried a clipboard. It presents a challenge, but the Judge trained me to utilize all my talents, and I have strived all my life to follow his wisdom." She hiccuped at me, then put her fingers on her lips and giggled. "It was most challenging to leave my country establishment without arousing unwanted attention."

"And how did you accomplish that?" I asked. As always, I supposed I ought to call Peter and share my discovery, but I was fascinated with her tale of exploits.

"In a laundry basket. It was unpleasant until I accustomed myself to the odor, and terribly uncomfortable. The laundry service is quite lax about leaving baskets in their vans; I must mention it to the matron so that she can speak to them."

"So you slipped out with the sheets in order to investigate," I prompted. "What have you been doing since then, besides avoiding an entire police department and attending school functions?"

"Would you like a cup of tea, Mrs. Malloy? I'm sure Tessa would not mind if we borrowed just a little and some water."

"No, no," I said hastily, "let's finish our chat before we indulge in—in tea. How did you learn that Miss Dort and Mr. Weiss were responsible for the errors in the journalism ledger?"

"The last letter to Miss Demeanor was, I fear, explicit. I turned quite pink at some of the language, but it was impossible to avoid the conclusion that the two were having some sort of relationship. The rest was obvious, wasn't it?"

After a fashion, and a week of reading old *Falcon Criers*. "Did you take the packet of letters from the school office?"

"Oh, my goodness, no. Although the letters should have been in the journalism mailbox, I happened to find them in Mr. Weiss's desk the afternoon of his funeral. I certainly did not take the letter in question with me as evidence; the Judge was very adamant about illegal search and seizure. However, I don't believe he ever gave an opinion from the bench about reading."

"You searched his desk, though."

"In the name of freedom of the press, my dear. The judge instilled in me a strong sense of priorities."

"How did you get into the building?"

"Mr. Pitts happened to be mopping the hallway and graciously let me inside. He even invited me to eat a meal with him, but I declined. Pizza is difficult to manage with dentures."

"You were in the school the afternoon Pitts died?" I said. "Did he mention anyone else in the building?"

"Pitts—died?" She turned white and put her hand on her chest. "I had no idea, no inkling of this. I feel quite stunned by the news. Mrs. Malloy, could you be so kind as to fetch me a glass of water?"

I went in the kitchen for water, then decided to hell with it and took the brandy bottle off the table. Once she was settled with a medicinal dose, her color improved to a pastel flush, if not a rosy glow. "You didn't know about Pitts?" I said.

"No, I am flabbergasted to hear of his death," she said. "I have not been able to watch the evening news, since I was worried someone might notice a light. Please tell me what happened to him."

"Let's discuss the murder of Herbert Weiss first. Were you aware that Miss Zuckerman spied on Pitts through the hole in the ladies room of the lounge, and overheard him selling certain information to Cheryl Anne?"

"She told me several days ago, but in the strictest confidence."

"Did she also mention that she laced your compote with Laetrile in order to poison him?"

Miss Parchester took a long drink of brandy, then looked up with a bleary smile. "Not in so many words, but I did wonder. I visited her classroom last night to see if her pills might be in a drawer, but I heard a policeman come down the stairs after me. I fled through the exit by the boiler."

"But you did know she had cancer, and had been to a Mexican clinic to try Laetrile—which is basically cyanide?"

"It seemed obvious."

The Judge had trained his daughter well, I told myself in an admiring voice. Or we had varying definitions of "obvious," with mine leaning toward "tentatively guessed after a week of ago-nized concentration."

"Tessa Zuckerman poisoned the peach compote and Herbert Weiss via a slight miscalculation, but she's been in the hospital since the day of the potluck. Who do you think murdered Pitts?" I asked her.

"I really couldn't say, Mrs. Malloy, I really couldn't say."

Damn. I'd been hoping it was obvious.

Miss Parchester announced that it was teatime, and went to the kitchen. I stayed in the living room with the brandy bottle, trying to work up enough enthusiasm to call Peter and inform him that I'd found his culprit. He wasn't apt to come roaring over with sirens and flashing lights, in that he knew she hadn't poisoned Herbert Weiss and her motive to murder Pitts was no stronger than anyone else's. Pitts hadn't been blackmailing Tessa Zuckerman, since she was unavailable for such things. He could have been blackmailing someone else, I thought tiredly, but it didn't seem likely. Blackmail requires secrecy; Pitts had been too eager to share his information.

Miss Zuckerman was the most promising candidate; she had admitted both motive and means, and the poison in the whiskey had also been an organic compound. She lacked opportunity, however. She was the only one who could not have left the whiskey for Pitts, I realized, sinking further into both the sofa and despair. Even Miss Parchester had visited the school, and had been invited for a cozy supper of pizza and whiskey. I wondered why her dear friend Tessa hadn't mentioned Pitts's death to her during one of their visits; Miss Parchester had been genuinely shocked when I told her.

I decided to ask her why, and went to the kitchen. The tea kettle was on the stove, but it wasn't whistling Dixie—or anything else. The cups and saucers were on the counter, along with a sugar bowl and two spoons. The back door was slightly open. Miss Parchester was thoroughly gone. It did not surprise me.

Once the tea things were put away and the African violets watered, I let myself out the front door and went to my car. I drove around the neighborhood for a few minutes, but I had little hope that I would spot her on the sidewalk, and I was proved right. Miss Zuckerman's house was located midway between the hospital and Farberville High School; I drove past both without success, then headed for home, aware that Miss Parchester would resurface in due time—probably disguised as a Maori, a nun, or a circus clown. Or all three, if she felt it necessary to operate as a tipsy, red-nosed, religious New Zealander.

As I unlocked my door, I heard the telephone ring. It was apt to be Peter, irate over Caron's lie and ready to bawl her out. Feeling as if I were trapped in a round of Russian roulette, I picked up the receiver. "I'm not available to come to the phone right now," I intoned. "At the sound of the —"

"Claire, this is Evelyn. I've just heard the most astounding news, and I presumed you'd be interested." When I agreed, she continued, "Jerry and Paula have had a major falling out. She came over to sob on my sofa and repeat numerous times how utterly horrid he was. It seems the coach and Miss Dort have come to an understanding: He's going to become administrative vice-principal, a position more in line with his credentials."

"But he'll get a raise, won't he? That puts the cottage and babies in the immediate future, which ought to delight her."

"I pointed that out to her, but she sobbed harder and said I didn't understand. I didn't, for that matter, but I couldn't get anything more from her." There was a long pause in which I supposed we were both mulling over the inexplicable turn of events. I was wrong. "Sherwood had good news," she said, sounding oddly hesitant.

"His manuscript has been accepted?"

"Yes, by a university press. He is, quite understandably, elated.

After a stream of *Gloria in excelsis*es and other incomprehensible utterances, he said the classics department there had an opening for an assistant professor next semester and wanted him to come immediately for an interview."

"That *is* good news," I said. "You don't sound especially thrilled, though."

"I guess I'll miss his conversations, as obscure and oppressively pedantic as they were. It's difficult to envision the same with Mrs. Platchett or Mr. Chippendale."

We chatted for a few more minutes, then I hung up and made myself a cup of tea. Cheryl Anne and Thud had parted ways, as had Jerry and Paula. Miss Dort's long-standing relationship with Herbert Weiss was finished, too, although not by choice of either participant. Evelyn and Sherwood might miss the obvious and end up at far ends of the educational spectrum. I wondered if Claire Malloy might be facing the same fate, due to a well-intentioned attempt to tidy things up and present Peter Rosen with a solution.

It was late in the afternoon by now, and said cop had not returned to chastise my daughter and listen to my latest bit of treachery. I wasted a few minutes chastising myself for losing Miss Parchester—for the umpteenth time, then took a piece of notebook paper and a pencil and sat down at the kitchen table. Charts and timetables had never worked yet, but one did cherish hope.

I listed all the names and drew arrows hither and yon. The paper began to look like a highway map, but I persevered until I had sorted out the relationships. I circled Sherwood's name as the only possessor of an illicit key, and Miss Zuckerman's as the possessor of a notably lethal bottle of tablets. I then underlined her name as the possessor of the most brazen motive. But she had been in the hospital, I reminded myself as I decorated the circle around her name with flowering vines.

But she did have loyal friends. Who were likely to visit that evening at seven o'clock.

I was staring at the paper when Caron and Inez slunk into the room. "Peter hasn't called or come by," I told the mendacious duo. "He will, of course, so you'd best call in Perry Mason to conduct your defense."

Caron put her hands on her hips. "You're the one who bungled things, Mother. Inez and I kept Miss Parchester on the line; you were supposed to find her and deliver her to the police."

"I did find her," I admitted, "but she managed to slip out the back door. There may be a way for us to redeem ourselves, however. I think she'll visit Miss Zuckerman this evening at the hospital. If you two—"

"No way," Caron said. She picked up her notebook and her purse, shot me an indignant look, and hobbled toward the door. "Inez and I are not about to stake out the hospital. The situation was totally humiliating. Come on, Inez, we're going to Rhonda's house. At least we won't be Tackled and Thrown to the floor there."

"What about your career?" I said. "It's possible that we can sort things out so that Miss Parchester can return to her classroom Monday morning, and the *Falcon Crier* can resume publication. You'll have the opportunity to write the Miss Demeanor column."

"I have decided to drop the journalism class. My design for the freshman class float won first prize; everyone agrees I have a talent. Therefore, I have decided to apply myself to set design in the drama department."

Inez bobbled her head. "And Rhonda heard that Rosie is over the mono and coming back to school next week." They limped out the door, discussing the Untimely Recuperation and the Lack of Consideration shown by certain parties.

I sat for a long time, then went into the living room and called

Peter. I listened to a lot of unkind words about my darling daughter and admitted the purpose of the ruse. I then admitted I'd lost Miss Parchester, but that I had a good idea when next we might find her. He skeptically agreed to meet me at the hospital at seven o'clock.

That left an hour. I wandered around the apartment for a while, visions of arrows dancing through my mind. I called Miss Dort again, and listened to the phone ring in vain, then snatched up my jacket and exited, although not with Caron's style.

There was a car in the parking lot at the high school. I tapped my car keys on the glass door, and Miss Dort subsequently appeared. The first time I'd gone through the routine, Miss Dort had been irritated to see me. This time she smiled as she held open the door; the Cheshire cat couldn't have looked more pleased with itself.

"Did you forget the yearbook layouts," she asked as we walked to the office, "or did you just want to work in peace? I do enjoy the school when the students are elsewhere. At times I think we could be more efficient if they simply stayed away, but that wouldn't work, would it?" She giggled at her heretical proposal.

"No," I said, bewildered by her behavior. "I wanted to ask you why you allowed Immerman to play in the Homecoming game. I realize it's none of my business, but I hoped you might tell me."

"I simply felt it was best for the school, although the Falcons failed to win the game. Immerman's not as important as he thought he was."

"I guess Jerry was disappointed," I said, beginning to get a glimmer of an idea. A decidely tacky idea. "After all, he made quite a bargain in order to get Immerman reinstated before the game."

Miss Dort patted her hair, if not her back. "An agreement was reached, but it had nothing to do with the issue of reinstatement.

Immerman was persuasive, and student morale is always upper-most in my mind."

"But you and the coach had quite a discussion."

"I called him in to inform him of my decision, but at that time I began to realize Coach Finley was much too valuable an asset to be left on a football field. Once we discussed the various directions his career might take, he agreed most readily to take on the position of administrative vice-principal."

"That's not what Weiss intended for him, is it?"

"Herbert wanted to have him fired, but he was afraid lest he alienate Miss Hart. He was biding his time until he could find a way to dispose of Coach Finley. Someone disposed of him in the interim."

I saw no reason to enlighten her. "You weren't caught in the same dilemma, Miss Dort. Offending Miss Hart surely is not your worst fear. Being alone on Thursday afternoons might be, however. Is that the bargain you made with Jerry—he stays on at Farberville High School, both as vice-principal and paramour?"

"I am getting older, Mrs. Malloy, and I have neither time nor inclination to join singles' clubs or prowl nightclubs. As acting principal of the school, I must maintain my standards."

"How persuasive was Immerman?"

"I fear it was a letter to Miss Demeanor that convinced me to let him play. Once I read it, I realized Cheryl Anne was the culprit, and quite vindictive enough to contact the school board with all sorts of misinformation about my little meetings with Herbert. She is incorrigible." Miss Dort gave me a tight smile. "To be succinct, Mrs. Malloy, she's a little bitch."

"That's how you discovered the identity of the poison-pen letter writer, isn't it? You took the packet of letters from the counter in the office. Sherwood and I searched the building for over an hour, but we couldn't find anyone."

"This is, as the students say, my turf. I suppose Herbert must have put the letters in his drawer and failed to mention it to me. It was most fortunate that you found them, Mrs. Malloy. They have since been destroyed."

"But Cheryl Anne and Immerman still know about the Xanadu. How can you be sure they won't use the information against you in the future?"

"Cheryl Anne is aware that I will report her blackmail scheme to the authorities should she try any more shenanigans. As for Immerman—we intend to discuss it on Tuesdays," she said. She settled her glasses on her nose, picked up her clipboard, and sailed out the office door.

A large percentage of my arrows had missed the target. Once I recovered from the shock and could move, I left the building and drove to the hospital, trying very hard not to dwell on the images that came to mind. Miss Dort would be caught eventually, and the school administration would not be impressed with her afternoon schedule. Thud was hardly a model of discretion, and Paula Hart was hardly the sort to give up gracefully. I was comforted with the knowledge that I would no longer be around the high school when the gossip started. Again. Rosie's journalistic integrity would be put to the test.

As I entered the hospital, I glanced around for undercover policemen and little old ladies in disguise but saw neither. Either I was wrong, or everyone was enjoying some degree of success. As I took the elevator upstairs, I prayed for the latter. Peter was waiting for me by the nurses' station.

"Miss Parchester can't possibly sneak in here," he said. "I've got men all around the building."

"She was here earlier this afternoon, apparently not too long after we were here. Did your men happen to notice her?" When he shook his head, I sweetly pointed out that she'd managed to avoid his men for a week, without having to miss any of her social obligations or school functions.

I was telling him about her escape from Happy Meadows when

Mrs. Platchett and Miss Bagby came out of the elevator. They acknowledged our presence with nods. We all trooped into Miss Zuckerman's room and positioned ourselves around the bed.

"How exciting to have so many visitors," she said. "It's almost a party, isn't it?"

"We're expecting one more," I said. "I think Miss Parchester will be here shortly."

The Furies exchanged looks. Mrs. Platchett at last cleared her throat and said, "Emily is a good and true friend, and she has been determined to spend as much time as possible with Tessa."

"Not that I have much time," Miss Zuckerman contributed. She looked at Peter. "I doubt you'll have an opportunity to arrest and detain me, Lieutenant, but I shall gladly sign a confession if that will assist you in your paperwork."

"For one murder—or for two?" I asked gently.

"Why, for two. I didn't intend to poison Mr. Weiss, but I seem to have done so anyway. I certainly intended to poison Mr. Pitts. I used exactly the same number of tablets."

"You couldn't have, Miss Zuckerman," I said. "You might have put the tablets in the whiskey, but you couldn't have taken it to the teachers' lounge and left it there."

She turned her head to one side. "But I did, Mrs. Malloy, and I insist on taking full responsibility."

At this point we heard a squeak outside the door. Peter and I stepped into a corner and watched as a green-clad orderly with a surgeon's cap and mask came into the room, pushing a wheelchair. It would have been more convincing if the orderly had not been wearing fuzzy pink slippers.

Mrs. Platchett and Miss Bagby tried to warn her, but Peter closed the door and positioned himself in front of it. "Miss Parchester, I'm Lieutenant Rosen of the Criminal Investigation Department. We've been looking for you."

"So I've noticed." She took off the cap and mask, then sat down in the wheelchair. "You really ought to speak to your men about their behavior, Lieutenant; it has bordered on police brutality. At times my civil liberties have been endangered by their youthful enthusiasm."

"We were discussing the identity of Pitts's murderer," I said as I came out of the corner. "Miss Zuckerman claims responsibility, but that's impossible."

"I did put Laetrile in the whiskey," Miss Zuckerman said in a firm voice that had stopped many a student in midstep. "I put one dozen tablets in the bottle. I would have put in a few more for good measure, but that was the last of them."

"Pitts was despicable," Mrs. Platchett said.

"He corrupted the students," Miss Bagby said.

"He had to be stopped," Miss Parchester added from the wheelchair. "Tessa's actions were warranted, even if they did violate his constitutional rights. The Judge was always harsh with criminals, especially those who were a threat to society."

Peter joined the circle around the bed. "But Miss Zuckerman did not buy the whiskey; someone else did and brought it to the hospital to be laced with poison. Someone then took it to the lounge where Pitts found and drank it. Either knowingly or unwittingly, one of you three ladies is an accomplice to murder."

The three looked back steadily, with nary a blink. One steely-eyed cop was no match for one hundred sixty collective years in the front of a classroom.

"One of you is guilty," he persisted, although with an increasing air of hopelessness. When he received no response, he looked at Miss Zuckerman. "Which one of your friends helped you murder Pitts?"

"If one of them is indeed an accomplice, she is guilty of no more than doing a small favor for a dying friend—and a major favor for the students of Faberville High School." She smiled, then closed her eyes and let her cheek fall against the pillow. We all tiptoed out of the room.

Miss Parchester announced that she needed to return the

wheelchair before it was missed. Miss Bagby opted to ride, and
the three squeaked toward the elevator, leaving an unhappy policeman and a bemused amateur sleuth in the hallway outside
Miss Zuckerman's room.

"Do you know which one did this 'small favor'?" he asked me.

"It doesn't really matter," I sighed. "Miss Zuckerman conceived and executed the plan; whoever delivered the bottle did so
for her. You're not exactly loosing a homicidal maniac on the
town."

He glanced at the closed door. "I suppose not, but what if
they decide they don't like the new custodian? They can't be
allowed to take matters into their own hands every time they
encounter a potential source of corruption in the corridors of the
school."

"Have a talk with them about retirement," I suggested. "I
doubt you'll get an argument, and the three of them can take a
nice bus tour of southern gardens in the spring. I'll check into
watercolor classes." Of the three, I was fairly certain Miss
Parchester needed the busiest schedule.

"I may check into Happy Meadows," he grumbled, but without heat. We walked out to his car and drove back to my apartment. I entertained him with an account of Miss Dort's
intentions, and the likelihood of retaliation from Paula Hart. The
teachers' lounge would continue to be a hotbed of gossip and
intrigue, I concluded as we went upstairs.

"But you won't have to be there, or take it upon yourself to
solve whatever mysteries arise," Peter murmured.

In that he was murmuring into my ear, I did not feel com-
pelled to point out that I had solved the murders for him. In the
midst of further murmurs, the telephone rang. It proved to be
Sherwood Timmons, bubbling with the news about his manuscript. I let him bubble for a minute or two, then interrupted
with congratulations.

"Thank you, dear sleuth," he said. "I shall cherish *ad infinitum* the memories of our minor escapade in crime."

"You had a key, even if it was an unauthorized copy," I reminded him. After all, Supercop was in my living room.

"I'll mail it to Miss Dort, accompanied by a note begging her forgiveness. She will make a terse note on her clipboard, but we will not have to listen to her crackly voice over the intercom or watch her lips purse with displeasure over——"

"We?" I inserted before he lost control of himself completely.

"Evelyn and I. I have proffered *vinculum matrimoniie,* and she has consented."

I congratulated him once more. After he said good-bye (*carpe diem,* actually, but I ignored it), I joined Peter on the sofa and told him about the impending *matrimoniie.* He gazed at me for a long time, looking terribly enigmatic. I opted for nonchalance.

"Claire," he at last said, "I can think of only one way to keep you out of trouble, and that's to——"

I stopped that nonsense. And with great charm, I might add.